B-BOY CHAMPIONSHIPS

FROM BRONX TO BRIXTON

DJ HOOCH

FOREWORD BY CR

10 9 8 7 6 5 4 3 2 1

First published in 2011 by Virgin Books, an imprint of
Ebury Publishing

A Random House Group Company

Text and photography copyright © DJ Hooch, 2011

The author has asserted his right under the Copyright,
Designs and Patents Act 1988 to be identified as the author
of this work.

www.randomhouse.co.uk

Address for companies within The Random House Group
Limited can be found at www.randomhouse.co.uk/offices.htm

The Random House Group Limited Reg. No. 954009

A CIP catalogue record for this book is available from the
British Library

ISBN 978-0-753-54001-5

The Random House Group Limited supports The Forest
Stewardship Council (FSC®), the leading international
forest certification organisation. Our books carrying the
FSC label are printed on FSC® certified paper. FSC is the
only forest certification scheme endorsed by the leading
environmental organisations, including Greenpeace. Our
paper procurement policy can be found at
www.randomhouse.co.uk/environment.

Designed by Lee Suttey at Visual Function_
Printed and bound in Italy by Printer Trento S.r.l.

To buy books by your favourite authors and register for
offers visit www.randomhouse.co.uk

THIS BOOK IS DEDICATED TO MY BEAUTIFUL LADY JULIA BELL.

It is additionally dedicated to my parents James and Sarah Whittle and to my brother Adam 'Ad-Funk' Whittle.

Hannah Knowles, thanks for all the work you put into this book, I know you went above and beyond to get this done.

In hip-hop we love to do big-ups and shout-outs, so in that tradition...

BIG UP:

All the b-boys & b-girls, poppers and lockers worldwide, it's your talent that pushes your dances to unbelievable levels and creates the occasion that is the UK B-Boy Championships. Over the past 15 years I have witnessed the passion and incredible skills you bring to all the battles and every year look forward to what new style and flava will be added to the history of this incredible event!

SHOUT OUTS:

Crazy Legs for taking a chance and agreeing to host the B-Boy Champs from the beginning and help guide its development and growth. Afrika Islam, you have been down with us since day one, always ready to rock the turntables at Funkin' Pussy parties and step up to co-host at the Champs giving us some of the most quoted lines along the way (Routine Routine!). Rob 'ChimpChilla' Pountney for working on keeping this ship moving, I know how hard you work. DJ Renegade, you're the oracle bro and the hardest working coach/dj/funny brotha out there. Thomas Hergenrother (Battle of the year), I appreciate your help since '96. Tyrone and Mario of 45 Live & IBE, you guys are the best, thanks for teaming up with us and helping to continue to build this thing worldwide. Johnjay & Charlie (Cartel Creative), thanks for bringing Korea to the Champs, we really have witnessed the explosion of Korean breaking first hand and you have so much to do with that; you definitely 'handled that'. Cros 1 (Armory Massive/Freestyle Session) thanks for always being down with the program. Takeo Miyata (Spartanic Rockers), your crew competing in '98 changed the Champs forever. Skeme Richards (Session 31), I love the music you spin and I promise to carry on tradition and meet you at the airport again. To Tha Dump, Jasper the vinyl junkie & Richard St Clair & the Funkin' Pussy sound squad, for over 10 years we party'd on the mothership and made history together.

Tuf Tim Twist (Rock Steady Crew), things ain't always been easy but we're still standing and 15 years' deep. B-Boy Mouse, you are one of funkiest dancers on the planet, keep on doing you little brotha. Tapeman, AK, Pete, K10 & Charlie, it isn't the Champs if A-shot ain't in the house. DJ James Leacy (RIP), we all miss you! David Jarvis (we go back a while now bro, ha), thanks for being part of this crazy journey, it really is no sleep till Brixton. Janine Douglas, thanks for all you help. Everyone at the Brixton Academy, the best venue in the world!

TO EVERYONE WHO CONTRIBUTED TO MAKING THIS BOOK, THANK YOU.

B-BOY CHAMPIONSHIPS: BRONX TO BRIXTON

BEFORE I BECAME A B-BOY, I WAS A KID FROM THE BRONX, WISHING I COULD HAVE THE OPPORTUNITY TO PLAY BASEBALL MORE OFTEN AND GO TO THE BOXING GYM, BUT THINGS LIKE THAT REQUIRED MONEY.

When I first came across b-boying in 1976, it was Afrika Islam and my brother Robert Colon dancing in front of where I lived; and I was completely embarrassed by what they were doing. This was before the word breakdancing existed so I had nothing to associate it with apart from the fact that my brother was throwing himself on the floor. I actually remember tucking my head down, thinking he was embarrassing my family by doing it.

A year later, I was brought to a jam by my cousin, Lenny Len, and that was the first time that I witnessed hip-hop fully-fledged. This was before it was even called hip-hop. There were b-boys and b-girls who were rocking and graffiti writers all over the place – in fact, they weren't called graffiti writers back then, just writers. So Lenny brought me to the jam and I saw all of this dancing going on; people on the microphone, all this energy, and I was blown away. I thought 'Wow, this is what I want to do.'

It was the first time I saw people getting down to break beats; the first time I understood what the neighbourhood really meant and what it represented. Being ten years old at that time was very exciting, because everything I wanted to do cost money, and everyone was out in the park doing *this* for free. The DJ and whoever owned the sound systems were taking a risk, because a lot of the time the people would get their sound systems taken away by the police, since they set up illegally in the park without a sound permit.

People say that hip-hop is a movement; hip-hop was never a movement – it was a party that evolved into a bunch of other things, and no one had any a clue that eight to nine years later people would see it as some sort of movement and label it hip-hop culture. This was just something we all did; we partied and we got down. Back then, you practised, you got better, you battled, you lost, you learned something new; you worked on it, developed it, battled again, you won or you lost – you kept going. For us it was all about how many people we could go out there and battle.

There was a crew called Rockwell Association that my cousin was in but they wouldn't let me in, because I was too young for them. Eventually this dude named Batch from TBB (The Bronx Boys) put me in his crew and I felt like I finally had a home, 'cos you didn't really come across solo b-boys back then, it was all about family: it was about bringing people together, bringing people from dysfunctional homes, from situations without any kind of social activity, to be involved in this. It brought us all together in a way that made us feel good about what we were doing. We would show up from one week to the next and bring something new to the game, taking things to the next level.

I guess the beauty of it was the innocence. If you were inspired to do something, there was no video, no YouTube or nothing; biting back then meant that you saw something and thought 'OK, I'm going to take this move, learn it and turn it in to something that I feel is mine and people are going to recognise my twist as well'. People had their own individuality and style. You wouldn't walk around looking like the next dude, or people were going to call you out on it, so biting wasn't as much of an issue; it was a whole different scene in those days.

The Bronx Boys and Rock Steady Crew were affiliates: TBB had RSC's back, and RSC had TBB's back. We were never a mixed crew; we always maintained the integrity of the name, but we were family. I got down with TBB in 1978 and with RSC in 1979. The Bronx Boys crew was huge – more like an organisation as opposed to a straight up b-boy crew – a bit like a Puerto Rican Zulu Nation. We wanted to be in a crew that was more like Rock Steady, so Lenny Len and I battled Jimmy Lee and Jimmy D: it wasn't about winning or losing (but, trust me, we wanted to win!), it was how you handled yourself and prepared for the battle. We lost the battle, but they were really impressed with the way we threw down. And that's what got us into Rock Steady Crew: we lost the battle but we gained their respect.

These days, all you have to do is be dope in order to get in a crew; you don't need to hang with the people the way you did back in those days. We didn't get into Rock Steady just based on the battle: we made it our business to be around them. If we heard they were going to be at whatever jam, we'd go chill with them, try and hang out with them, even if they didn't f***ing talk to us, even if they treated us like s***. We paid our dues, the hard way. And once you were accepted, it was nothing but love and respect.

By the time we got into Rock Steady Crew, the breaking was starting to die. We got in too late, on one level, but on another we got in at just the right time: we became the people to save the dance. I started developing all these moves that were mine, and we started travelling all around the city, just to find people that we could battle. At the time, and at the age we were, travelling around the city was like travelling around the world. I just wanted to battle people, and make Rock Steady the biggest crew in the city. After Zulu Nation there was no other crew that was bigger than us. And along the way when we battled people, we indirectly contributed to the scene getting better, 'cos some of those people that were in RSC thought that Rock Steady was too big, and they wanted to be involved with something else, so they started their own crews; several b-boys from New York City Breakers started as members of Rock Steady Crew or another crew as well. It was a breeding ground for other crews.

After moving to Manhattan for a few years and losing touch with members of Rock Steady Crew, I found myself continuing on a mission to seek out more people to battle, teach and hang out with, based on our mutual interest in getting better and battling. Rockwell Association saw me taking things to another level and they allowed me to start a chapter in Manhattan, but when I saw Jimmy D again, I told that I'd rather be doing it for Rock Steady Crew – so he gave me a Rock Steady Crew chapter, and six months later he gave me the whole thing, in 1981.

Around the same time, Henry Chalfant (photographer and videographer) wanted to see what we were doing and started involving us with things going on in the downtown scene – and started documenting us. When it comes to the media industry, Henry discovered Rock Steady Crew. He's the one that brought us out to the rest of the world and it was truly innocent; truly without the intention of capitalising off us financially, which was a beautiful thing. So we owe so much to Henry Chalfant. We got together with Henry to do one of the first hip-hop shows produced. The first ever show produced was called *Graffiti Rock*, in '81, which Michael Holman later used the same name for a television pilot. We did the show for Henry Chalfant at Common Ground, SoHo, New York. And that was really what exposed hip-hop to the world. It was the first time hip-hop was ever presented as a culture. Although we were not calling it hip-hop yet, it was the first time the four primary elements (DJing, MCing, graffiti, b-boying) were put on display for a community outside of our own. It wasn't called hip-hop until 1982. And Afrika Bambaataa gets full credit for the naming of it.

We were already getting press in various magazines that were out in Europe, and we had already done a documentary called *Portfolio* with Antonio Lopez (*Fashion Illustrator*), who started quite a few careers. Probably that, as well as the Rock Steady Crew documentary that was done by 20/20 Films Ltd., was the first thing to give us some shine. And some point then Malcolm McLaren came in and put us in the Buffalo Girls video, which took us to another level.

We didn't feel different with this international success: we were just some little b***ards getting high on road, just acting up. It was all about the party. And when we danced, we really didn't give a s*** about what the people thought – we just wanted props from each other. It wasn't for the sake of having a career: we had no clue, we didn't give a s***. We were kids, we weren't cultured, and didn't know where we were going with this: we had a stereotype about everything and everywhere we were going, so we really had no respect for a whole bunch of s***: we had no appreciation for what we were doing.

That wave of fame started to die out around '86, though I believe that was only in the States. In Europe and Japan there were a lot of things going on, although they weren't able to get the press that we had. It wasn't the case that we stopped and everyone else stopped. In the US, though, we were basically shunned – one minute we were these ghetto celebrities, walking to the front of the line at the club, the next thing you know, we were sent to the back of the line: hip-hop was changing. What was the golden era of hip-hop for some people out there wasn't really golden for us b-boys.

Since we had no way to mass-produce ourselves at the time, we got lost in the shuffle. So years later I started putting b-boy videos (Bootleg Betty) out there and people started sharing them as well. No one was bootlegging themselves at the time, and it led to people making videos of themselves and their crews or events: that and people being hungry to go off and battle helped the rebirth of breaking when we thought it was dead for a second time. Without question, if it weren't for the fact that Rock Steady Crew got back involved, it wouldn't have gone down the way it did; you gotta give props to Fabel, Wiggles, Ken Swift, and everyone else that did their thing in order to revive their skills or coming out as something new.

In the '90s some dude named Hooch hit me up and asked me to host the UK 'Breakdance' Championships. I had an issue with the name of the event and brought it to his attention – Hooch eventually changed the name, props to him, for trusting me. At that time, we (RSC) were in the process of trying to recreate what we were doing as something new, so we remembered that we didn't call what we did 'breakdance'. In the early days we called it rocking, we called it going off, we called it breaking and b-boying. We brought the term b-boy back to protect the integrity of our history. People were very apprehensive when it came to the reconditioning of and use of the term b-boy. A lot people that had no clue about the history of this dance thought they knew more than they actually did when it came to what was right or wrong. And there was a lot of hate, but that was something I was willing to accept, 'cos I was on a mission. When I was a judge at the UK Champs, I had to deal with being booed, because I was dealing with an audience that only wanted to see the acrobatic element of the dance and not the elements that made it a dance. They were like 'Nah, that can't be, 'cos he just spun on his head a million times' and I'd think, 'Yeah, he just spun on his head a million times, but he never danced: he never did something that is required to make it dance, one of them being rocking to the beat'.

The presentation of what hip-hop was, and the terms that described it, were changed by the UK media and Kool Lady Blue (our first manager). We didn't say the words breakdance when we first started performing; it wasn't in our lingo. The same way I don't have the right to rename anything coming from someone else's community, I don't think anyone else should have the right to come into something they are not part of and rename it for the sake of easy understanding by outsiders. So we decided to lead the way and research why and what was wrong, then we made people aware. After that, it was up to them to do the right thing in order to protect hip-hop.

My experience with the Champs has ultimately been about the direction that Hooch as a promoter has taken, in terms of educating people and being in line with what hip-hop really is; I think the UK Champs is a great success for hip-hop as a whole – there is no denying the fact that Hooch is the f***ing man in the UK, and to deny the UK B-Boy Championships is actually subtracting from hip-hop. This is about impact, and the importance of what the UK B-Boy Champs is towards sustaining hip-hop.

There's a stark difference when you compare what Hooch does, and what other people are doing in Europe; some people are continuing the false education of what hip-hop is. A lot of people in Germany know what real hip-hop is, a lot of people in Korea know what real hip-hop is, a lot of people in France know what real hip-hop is – but the promoters (United States as well) keep perpetuating the stuff that was wrong by continuously putting it out there as fact, and when it comes to what we do as an art form they're scared to go against the grain. Hip-hop has always gone against the grain; real hip-hop that is.

Being on stage with Afrika Islam at the Champs, has been a great experience. Afrika Islam was there at the time of my first experience in hip-hop, so to have him on stage with me and introducing me as one of the original b-boys was a great thing. One of the most memorable experiences was going from being booed by the UK audience to eventually having them clapping for my decisions – and now being an educated audience that attends (sometimes better than the judges). That, to me, is the best, because it's like I go out there and the audience *gets* it – they know, and that in itself, more than anything – an educated hip-hop crowd – is a beautiful thing. And we did that together.

Crazy Legs

INTRODUCTION

THE BATTLE TO END ALL BATTLES

B-BOYING – THE ORIGINAL DANCE OF HIP-HOP CULTURE – IS A BATTLE DANCE. FROM ITS INCEPTION IT HAS BEEN A WAY OF SETTLING SCORES AND PROVING YOUR SKILLS ARE BETTER THAN OTHERS' WITHOUT FIGHTING.

DJ Hooch

B-boy Brahim, Pokemon crew, in battle mode.

In New York in the 70s there were serious gang problems. Afrika Bambaataa, a DJ from the South Bronx and legendary figure in the hip-hop world, was a major gang leader, but he saw the need to get away from violence. He realised the way forward could be through using the culture of hip-hop – DJing, MCing, b-boying and graffiti; where the rivalries could be positive.

Afrika Bambaataa founded one of the first b-boy crews, the Zulu Kings, but the name b-boy was given to the dancers by DJ Kool Herc (widely credited as the founder of hip-hop music) because the dancers originally danced to the breaks of the tracks he was playing and thus became break boys or 'b-boys'. Groups of dancers came together to form crews, practising and spending hours a day creating incredible new moves and crew routines.

The Rock Steady Crew was one of the first professional b-boy crews travelling the world performing shows and battling – and probably had more fame than any other crew. They influenced the dancing with their recognised style, technical moves and their desire to keep the Rock 'Steady'. As this first wave of breaking was exploited in the media, they very quickly became global stars.

The spread of b-boying across the world has developed into an explosion in recent years. Worldwide, b-boying was answering the call from young people looking for something to do, that wasn't coming from the media, wasn't controlled by big corporations, wouldn't cost them anything to do, and was something they could do anywhere. There's a simplicity to breaking that makes it accessible to people all over the world – especially to people without much money.

There's a particularly strong resonance with b-boy culture at the moment. We still have real problems with gang activity and mindless violence: the kids only realise it when they're older and may have wasted their lives, but with something to channel their energy into there is another future. This is a culture that kids all over the world can relate to, which the internet has proved.

The internet has had a huge impact on b-boying – now people can search for their favourite dancers and see who's doing what. Battles that happen today will have footage online by tonight. There's a global community talking to each other, networking, sharing ideas, rating different dancers and crews. In this new global age, b-boys and b-girls now have fans; fans who may not be involved in breaking or any element of hip-hop themselves, but are fans of the dance. Millions of people watch it on YouTube, Facebook and other social networks. It's all fed into an explosion of b-boying.

It's not a new culture - it's been around for 35 years, but the underground perception is starting to give way to a new sense of awareness for the potential of the top dancers to become stars. The new generation of b-boys is recognized more as extreme athletes, like top skateboarders, with endorsement deals and pro careers. The skill level is so high now, that you can't be the best overnight. You have to do it for years to be at the top. If you want to be the 'illest in the game' you have to live it, you've got to be 100% committed.

Salah, France

B-BOYING/BREAKING

A form of street dancing, originally performed to the breakdown sections of the record, which incorporates top rock, footwork, power moves and freezes. In the 80s it was referred to as breakdancing.

B-BOY/B-GIRL

Break boy or break girl - a breaker who 'lives' the lifestyle and is dedicated to the art form.

BATTLE

A dance-off between different solo dancers or crews, which can be at a staged competition or in cyphers.

BITER

A biter is someone who copies another b-boy/b-girl's moves or style instead of doing their own thing.

COMBOS/COMBINATIONS

A series of different moves put together in a sequence.

CREW

A group of b-boys / b-girls who dance and battle together. Some crews are formed locally whilst others have a more international line-up.

CYPHER

A circle where dancers throwdown, sometimes just jamming to the music and other times in battle.

FLOORWORK/DOWNROCK

This includes all footwork and variations performed on the floor, including the foundational 6-step.

LOCKING

A style of street dance originating from LA, California. Started by Don Campbell in the late '60s.

POPPING

Style of dancing in which the body jerks as the dancer contracts and relaxes muscles quickly, called a 'pop'. This is done continuously to the beat of the track, and incorporates different moves and poses.

POWER MOVES

These are actions that require momentum and physical power to execute. Examples of these include the Windmill, Swipe, Flare and Airflare.

ROUTINE

A series of moves that are connected in practised sequences by two or more dancers, and often involving full crews.

SMOKED

When a dancer 'gets smoked', he has been totally beaten by his opponent in a way that leaves no doubt who the winner is.

TOPROCK

Steps performed from a standing position. This is usually the opening display of style.

STYLE/FLAVA

The best dancers and crews have their own style, or flava - their own individual personality as a dancer that marks them out. It's not just about technique - if you haven't got your own style you're not going to stand out.

DANCERS' STORIES

EVO (STEPHEN EVANS), UK

SOLO B-BOY CHAMPION, 1996, 1997, 1998; STREET MACHINE CREW

Manchester is my hometown and where I started dancing. I first hit the floor, or grass at the time, around 1983 after getting the buzz from listening to my brothers' mix-tapes and through dancing around where I lived: in the chippies, outside, at friend's, etc. A well-known older guy from my area spotted me throwing down on some grass near my house and that was the beginning.

I would hit all the shopping centres, jams, etc, meeting various fresh and innovative dancers along the way who helped me to train harder and try to be better, so I could bounce my way up the crew hit list. I trained hard when I needed to, sometimes getting up in the middle of the night to master a move...

The things that inspired me to start breaking are all the things that drive us: music, anger, love... The old days in Manchester were the best for me. Battles were not just dancing; there was fighting in the early years. Having been a b-boy has give me an opportunity to see the world and also meet many amazing people, and I believe my hard training paid for that.

I had the chance to show what I could at the Champs, and by the time I last battled there had established myself in the game. These days the French stand out a bit because they have the 'I don't give a f*** idea', but there are a lot of new kids out there.

I never analyse dancing that much - some people just stand out. It all falls into place.

MOVES

B-boy Flea Rock

TOP ROCK

AN INTEGRAL AND IMPORTANT PART OF B-BOYING. IT'S HOW YOU ENTER THE BATTLE; IT'S THE STAND-UP PART OF THE DANCE BEFORE YOU GET DOWN OR DO ANY FOOTWORK. ATTITUDE IS KEY, AND SHOWING YOUR CHARACTER.

DROP/GET DOWN

THE TRANSITION FROM TOP ROCK TO DOWNROCK/
FOOTWORK OR MOVES. KUDOS IS GIVEN FOR HOW
UNEXPECTED THE GET-DOWN IS.

B-boy Kid Glyde

FOOTWORK/DOWNROCK

FOOTWORK IS MADE UP OF THE DIFFERENT
LEGWORK PATTERNS PERFORMED ON THE
FLOOR, USUALLY IN A CIRCULAR PATTERN; IT
INCLUDES VARIOUS NUMBERED STEPS, CC'S,
SWITCHES, SWEEPS, ETC. THE HANDS SUPPORT
THE DANCER AS MUCH AS THE FEET.

FREEZE/S

YOU USUALLY COME INTO A FREEZE FROM SOME FORM OF MOVEMENT. IT'S THE PUNCTUATION OF THE DANCE AND IS EXACTLY WHAT IT SAYS – THE DANCER FREEZES; OFTEN SUSPENDED OFF THE GROUND SUPPORTED BY HAND/FOOT. SOMETIMES USED AS A TRANSITION.

MOVES

THESE ARE ACTIONS THAT REQUIRE MOMENTUM AND PHYSICAL POWER TO EXECUTE; THEY ARE ACROBATIC MOVES, WHICH REQUIRE STRENGTH, CONTROL AND AGILITY. THEY GENERALLY USE THE BODY CORE TO SUPPORT THE MOVES OF THE LEGS.

Flea Rock

THESE INCLUDE:

POWER MOVES
BACK SPINS
WINDMILL
TURTLE SWIPES
HEAD SPIN
1990S/2000S

AIR MOVES
FLARE
AIR FLARES
CHAIR FLARES
STAR TRACKS

TRICK MOVES
AIR CHAIR
HIGH CHAIR
HAND HOPS
FLIPS

B-Boy Differ, T.I.P. crew (Korea).

1990 (90S)

WHERE A B-BOY PERFORMS A FAST-SPINNING ONE-HANDED HANDSTAND, ROTATING 360°. THE RECORD FOR THE MOST 90S IN ONE GO IS 30, HELD BY ITALIAN B-BOY, CICO (SEE PHOTOS). THE NAME ORIGINATES FROM THE EIGHTIES – IT WAS CALLED 1990S BECAUSE THE MOVE WAS SEEN AS SO FUTURISTIC. 2000S ARE THE TWO-HANDED VERSIONS.

ATTITUDE

ATTITUDE

IT'S NO GOOD HAVING THE MOVES AND TECHNIQUE IF YOU DON'T HAVE THE ATTITUDE TO STAND OUT. THE TOP B-BOYS AND B-GIRLS HAVE THEIR OWN STYLE (FLAVA), AND THAT'S NOT JUST ABOUT SIGNATURE MOVES; IT'S HOW THEY STAMP THEIR PERSONALITY ON A BATTLE.

B-Boy Ryoma, Mortal Kombat (Japan).

B-boy Ivan, the urban action figure.

Above: Alien Ness (Zulu Kings) and below: Roxy (Soul Mavericks) show their swagger.

DANCERS' STORIES

JUNK (JOHN ISAACS), UK

CREW: SECOND TO NONE
WORLD CREW CHAMPION, 1996, 1997

Seeing lads at the local under-18s disco doing body popping in 1984, then seeing later movies Breakdance and Beat Street made me get into dancing. I guess the first time I was in what I could call a real battle (there would always be a competitive element in the circle with your other breakers) we were at a Chaka Khan concert in Poole in 1985. There were breakers from some other town and a battle circle started. I was very nervous, of course. I had just recently learnt the windmill but I didn't have the courage to do it as I feared I might mess it up. I did my hand-glide instead and did it well, which I felt pleased about, but disappointed I didn't do a windmill as no one else did a windmill in the circle. In 1985 a windmill was a very special move.

B-boying has been a very positive experience for me. Whilst growing up it gave me a lot of confidence. I was very shy in my early teens but having to overcome the fear of dancing in a circle with everyone watching you certainly gets you over your shyness. Breaking also got me fit. Before I started breaking I had no interest in sport and therefore did no physical activity. Breaking changed all that and I became extremely fit from breaking. I think as you get older (I'm 41 now) it keeps you in shape, which is very important as your metabolism naturally slows down, so the exercise you get helps to stop that. I've also travelled all over the UK and Europe, been on tv and in music videos lots of times, met lots of famous people and been to some amazing events. Things I would have never experienced had I not done it. I also met my wife Yasmin through breaking.

Being in a crew – I'm in Second to None – or an informal group to train is important, as you need others to dance with to motivate you. It's hard to do it alone all the time. At my peak I used to train nearly every day and for hours and hours. We had places we would go on a regular basis and I would rarely miss a session. I don't do it so often now as I don't always have the energy or am too busy, but I have got a dance studio I built in my garden, which makes it much easier to train more regularly.

Technique is the key to all power-moves: if you haven't got the technique right then the move won't work. Strength is not essential but a good strength to weight ratio is essential. If you are light then you do not need to be that strong, but if you are heavy then you will need to be stronger. If you are heavy and weak then you will struggle, if you are light and strong it will be easy. On top of that you need to feel the beat to make the whole thing funky. Without that it would be gymnastics and not a dance.

I like really rough break-beats and grooves for breaking to. Often with the tracks these break-beats come from, the track played in its entirety isn't suitable to break to, so the break part needs either to be looped on a sampler/computer or double decked live to keep just the break part going.

I always loved the Champs when I was taking part – being a spectator is not so good for me, being a dancer, but it's still great. I must admit to being a little out of touch with the present scene but I always thought the Americans had nice style, and I personally feel that having a good style is the most important thing with breaking.

INSPIRATIONS:

Robert Kiyosaki.

FAVOURITE DJ:

I always thought 'Clark Kent' is one of the best hip-hop DJs for playing a set you can dance to. His mixing combined with double decking is so perfected, but he does not go over the top with scratching and double decking, which is important to b-boying. Turntableism is a very highly skilled art form in its own right but you cannot break to a competition turntableism set.

BATTLES

LET THE BATTLE BEGIN....

I STARTED RUNNING MY CLUB NIGHT, 'FUNKIN' PUSSY', AT THE BEGINNING OF 1992 AS LONDON WAS EMERGING FROM THE HAZE OF ACID HOUSE.

The club was always packed! The b-boys cyphered at the back of the hall.

Playing a mixture of hard funk beats and up-tempo hip-hop, the club launched at a basement venue called The Fish (previously known as Spatz), which was a mecca for b-boys in the 80s, when Tim Westwood hosted his Saturday afternoon jams there.

In 1994 we moved the night to the Africa Centre in Covent Garden, and it was around this time that the b-boys started to hit the club. Because we were getting more breakers coming to the club, we thought we'd do an event for them at the centre, but this quickly developed into the blueprint to host an official b-boy championships. There were no big, organised events for b-boys in the UK at the time and there was clearly a hunger for one.

I had a music promotion background, so I knew how to put on a show, and because of my club background I knew the vibe the event needed to have. The difference between a club night and a championship event would be the venue – and having a legend hosting it. Who else to approach but Crazy Legs from the Rock Steady Crew? The Rock Steady Crew were doing a show off Broadway called 'Jam on the Groove', so it looked like Crazy couldn't do the Championships. But as luck would have it (for us), it turned out he was injured so I left him details about what I was planning for the Championships.

A month later I got a call at five in the morning from Legs. 'Don't call it breakdancing!' was his first response, and that it should be called 'b-boying.' At the time it wasn't commonly known as b-boying over here, so I suggested Crazy should come over, host the Championships and re-educate us.

Gradually crews started signing up to compete at the Champs – and I secured appearances by rap legends Schoolly D and the London Posse. Shepherd's Bush Empire was the venue booked for the first Champs. They looked at us like we were crazy when we said what we intended on staging there and said they'd give us the downstairs space, which was for 750 people. In the end 1,500 people turned up! Right from the start we knew something was happening because we were immediately invited on to the *Big Breakfast* on Channel 4, mentioned in the style mags, and had lots of national media interest.

The first year featured crews from the UK, plus one crew from Denmark. The Prodigy, who were in the audience, took the winner of the solo competition, b-boy Evo, along with Tim Twist of the Rock Steady Crew and DJ Leacy on their stadium tour and they also used a photo from the Championships for the 'Smack My Bitch Up' single cover. By the time we moved to Brixton Academy in 1998, the event had become truly international, with crews from the UK, US, Japan, Germany and Denmark.

Although we weren't aware of it at first, we were part of a renaissance in b-boying worldwide. We started the event because we thought it would be a good thing to do, not to create a global scene – we knew other countries had scenes that were growing stronger and it came at the right time. People have come to the B-Boy Champs and fed off the incredible atmosphere, inspiring them to get involved with the culture and some to create their own events. Now the Championships has qualifiers in countries all over the world.

The b-boys come to the competition to win and to be seen as the best. Today, thanks to endorsements and being involved in films, music videos and tours, there's a growing number of dancers now making a living out of b-boying. Until the Championships the b-boys were completely unknown outside the culture, and now some of these guys are becoming global superstars. In the following pages – along with introductions to the different battles – you can see them in action.

POPPING IS THE DANCE OF 'HITTING' YOUR MUSCLES TO THE BEAT OF THE MUSIC TO CREATE A SNAPPING EFFECT. IT INVOLVES FUNK, ILLUSION, MIME AND MUSICALITY AND CREATES AN AMAZING SPECTACLE OF STANDING DANCE. THE TOP INTERNATIONAL LINE-UP SETS THE STAGE FOR SOME AWESOME BATTLES.

The success and popularity of the World Popping Battle make it one of the most eagerly anticipated competitions. This battle always displays incredible dance skills from eight of the world's best.

Popula, USA, sporting more traditional Popping attire.

Left: Salah (France), deep in thought before battle and, *above*, in action.

Walid (France): one of the most respected poppers of all time, performing his judge's solo in 2004.

DANCERS' STORIES

DEYDEY (DELPHINE NGUYEN), FRANCE:

POPPING CHAMPION, 2009

I started dancing aged eight – hip-hop and new jack swing. In 2001, a big crew from Paris and Poppin Taco came to my hometown to teach workshops and something just clicked. That's when I decided to specialise in funk styles (Popping and Locking). I grew up the hard way, in what we call 'Cité' in French (ghetto). Dancing was a way to keep me busy and out of trouble. I spent my teenage years practising every day – I didn't have time for boys or that kind of thing!

I was the first woman to enter the B-Boy Champs, in 2007, and the first to win, in 2009. The first time, just entering was an amazing chance to show my skills and prove girls could be as good as the guys. The second time, I was going through a tough time personally, so I got into warrior mode! I was nervous, because I was representing France – and women – and wanted to prove I could do it. I won the first two battles, but wasn't happy with how I danced and thought, I'll show you tomorrow! The second day arrived and the vibe was great, with lots of energy from the audience. The first round was against Hozin (Korea). I thought, either I'll get smoked or I have to win. After seeing his round to a Michael Jackson song, I knew I was going to win.

In the final against Slim Boogie (USA), with the French dancers behind me, I felt strong. When I heard the beat from Renegade I thought, I'm going to kill it! Winning was a dream come true. When I won Juste Debout (the biggest upright street-dance-styles competition in the world) in 2010, I felt I proved that my victory at the UK Champs wasn't luck, but skills.

INSPIRATIONS:

My big sister Cathy, Electric Boogaloos, Smiley, Walid, Bruce... I dedicate this to my dad, RIP.

Shoon Boog (USA), son of Popin' Pete, of the the legendary Electric Boogaloos.

Nelson, en route to winning the 2010 World Popping title.

Djidawi, 2009 semi-finalist: one of the new generation of poppers coming out of France.

Salah's amazing flexibility sets him apart from other dancers.

DANCERS' STORIES

SALAH (SALAH BENLEMQAWANSSA), FRANCE:

CREW: VAGABONDS
POPPING CHAMPION, 2006; WORLD CREW CHAMPION, 2010

I was inspired to start dancing when I saw the O Posse crew dancing in the street, and started at a famous place in Paris called the Trocadero in 1995.

I entered my first battle with Mohamed, leader of Vagabond Crew and ex-member of The Family. We were in Miami Beach, and there was a small dancing competition. We lost in the final, but it was funny because the audience was so angry at the decision they booed the organiser and threw plastic chairs at the judges!

B-boying, popping, locking and other forms of dance are my medicine. It's the place I can express myself. I was so shy before, and dancing changed me.

Being with the Vagabond Crew really taught me a lot. Mohamed Belarbi, the leader of Vagabonds, taught me how to be a teacher and really structure my dance. He explained so many good strategies for battling – as did Karim from Actuel Force, Junior Almeda and other dancers. But those are my secrets!

I've dedicated my life to training – if I'm not dancing I go to the gym; if I don't dance or go to the gym I'm thinking of how to create a new show or develop a new style of dancing.

The Championships have been some of the best memories of my life – I'll never forget winning the 2010 crew final with Vagabond Crew.

DANCERS' STORIES

JSMOOTH (JAY GUTIERREZ), USA

CREW: MACHINE GONE FUNK
WORLD POPPING CHAMPION, 2006

I started popping about 10-11 years ago - I'd been inspired by Poppin Taco on the movie *Breakin'* and my big brother Damion (RIP). I remember some of my first battles... I was wack though and lost - I was rushing through all my movements. I did Pro AM in 2003. Terrible. I drank two coffees and that made me worse. The first time I started battling right and was fearless was in 2004 at the B-Boy Summit vs Salah. No one knew anything about me - I didn't win anything major or get to any major finals but I brought it to Salah. I didn't care who he was; I just wanted to do me. He clowned on me bad but I still kept coming! That was a fun and memorable first good battle.

Popping is my life. I wake up and breathe the dance. I never stop thinking, day-dreaming and practising; while I'm driving in my car; while I'm walking to the store; while I'm trying on new clothes; when I go shopping... Everything I do involves dance. I've been able to see the world, and been to places I thought I'd never go. It's a blessing.

I'm a member of Machine Gone Funk. Being a part of a crew just makes your dance stronger because you can vibe with people who inspire you. When I train it's usually a case of just getting down and working on something specific. If I feel like popping hard that day I'll try to work on different hitting techniques within the freestyle, or if I feel like waving I'll try to take that as far as I can.

Technique makes you clean, and clean means it's more visually powerful for people watching you. It's definitely important to me: I like to watch clean dancers. Musicality should be natural; you shouldn't have to try too hard, it should just be inside you. I like to get down to 80s funk - funk with feeling!

I won in the popping battle in 2006 - I was the first solo American to win that battle at the Champs and I am still the only one! In 2007 I had an amazing battle against Salah. I thought I won that one, but hey, the judges chose otherwise. In 2008 I was a judge. Every time was amazing; just being on stage and being a part of this great event.

LOCKING

THIS FUNKY STOP AND START DANCE CALLED LOCKING WAS CREATED BACK IN THE LATE 60S BY DON CAMPBELL AND PIONEERED BY THE DANCE GROUP 'THE LOCKERS'. THE WORLD'S BEST PAIRS BATTLE IT OUT TO SEE WHO IS THE FUNKIEST ON THE PLANET.

Locking is probably the least well known of the streetdances, so expect to be surprised by some incredible dancing, some incredible routines, as well as some incredible outfits!

P-Lock and Jimmy Soul vs. the GoGo Brothers was one of the all-time epic locking battles, with subsequent YouTube views in the millions.

P-Lock, France

Jimmy Soul, France

Atomic Splitz, Japan, in battle against LMC, lockers from Cyprus.

Upside down you're turning me: A-Train and Razzle Dazzle from Sweden: locking champions, 2009.

Flocky and Rae (Germany), en route to taking the locking title against the Bitter Box Sisters of Japan (*right*), 2010. Their trademark routines brought huge roars of appreciation from the Brixton crowd.

Lock it up: Lockadelic (*left*) and Scramble Lock of France and Canada.

IN EVERY CREW BATTLE THERE'S ALWAYS ONE DANCER WHO STANDS OUT, THEIR SUPERSTAR. SOME HAVE MORE THAN ONE. THE SOLO BATTLE OFFERS UP THE FLOOR, EXCLUSIVELY, FOR THESE B-BOY GALACTICOS.

There's nobody just making up the numbers: none but the very best can take part; they are the gladiators of the floor. The world's best breakers from all over the globe battle it out, one-on-one, to establish who is the supreme b-boy.

Freeze!: Robin of Top 9 crew, Russia, holds his classic freeze.

Japanese b-boy catching air.

B-boy Leo (Germany), hand-hopping.

B-boy Komer, Russia (Top 9 Crew), shows his style.

Beebish (France) rockin' her footwork.

DANCERS' STORIES

PHYSICX (KIM HYO KEN), KOREA

CREW: RIVERS
SOLO B-BOY CHAMPION, 2004;
WORLD CREW CHAMPION, 2002, 2004, 2005

I remember the first time that I saw b-boying, but it's hard to express in words. The moves simply shocked me. I just knew deep in my heart that this was the path I was going to take. For me, b-boying is a way of life: every amazing experience I get from b-boying gives me satisfaction.

It's been 16 years since I started dancing – half my life. My first battle was probably back in 1998. I battled with a crew that was from a different city. Back in the day I used to be very confident about my technique and it gave me great pleasure that it made me stand out.

Today I'm with the Rivers Crew. Every individual in Rivers Crew has a different style, but at the end of the day we all want the same thing: all of us want to become a great technician. I don't even want to imagine my life without Rivers Crew. As much as I'd like to practise everyday, I can't – for personal reasons – but do carry out regular practice sessions.

There are amazing b-boys all over the world. However, recently this b-boy called Lil G from Venezuela left quite an impression on me. He was in very good physical condition and the energy he was generating was off the hook; the type of energy that I haven't felt for a long time – he reminded of me when I was young.

UK B-Boy Championships 2002 was the first international event that I participated in. It had a huge impact on my b-boy career. I was very lucky to have had the experience, thanks to Johnjay and Charlie from Cartel Creative.

INSPIRATIONS:

Bruce Lee. My favourite DJs are DJ Element and DJ Muro.

MOUSE (ERESON ORTEGA CATIPON), UK/PHILLIPINES:

CREW: FLOORGANGZ
SOLO B-BOY CHAMPION, 2006

I started b-boying when I moved to England from the Philippines – about 15 years ago – inspired by the people involved in it, and the culture. Plus I'm a show-off, and this is the best way to show off and express yourself!

My first battle was in Birmingham. I was in a club minding my own business, just trying to fit in because I'd just got to England. They were playing old skool beats – I think it was a Bambaataa record. I saw some b-boys – Tuff Tim and the Stoke-on-Trent b-boy crew called Under Attack. Well, I didn't know them at all, but I could see they were exchanging moves, so I thought I could jump in.

Every time I tried to jump in they blocked me. I thought, if I can't join them, I will make them join me, and it worked like a charm. I started on them, busting out moves that I knew. They all turned round and start attacking the floor, one by one. I was 16 years old and scared and excited at the same time. The feeling was electric. I just kept going, even though I didn't know what I was doing. As long as I had peeps cheering, I was in!

You're supposed to have one crew and stick to it for better or worse, and I'm all for that, but sometimes it's not easy if you can't relate to everyone. Now I'm in Floorgangz, a crew from six countries. When I joined, it was the first time I felt someone had my back. The effect on me is huge – every one of them is dope, so I have to keep busy and keep surprising them with new s***!

B-boying has opened my eyes to so much and taught me that everything is possible – as long as you work for it and put your all into it, life will reward you in the long run.

INSPIRATIONS:

James Brown, Frosty Freeze and innovative DJs.

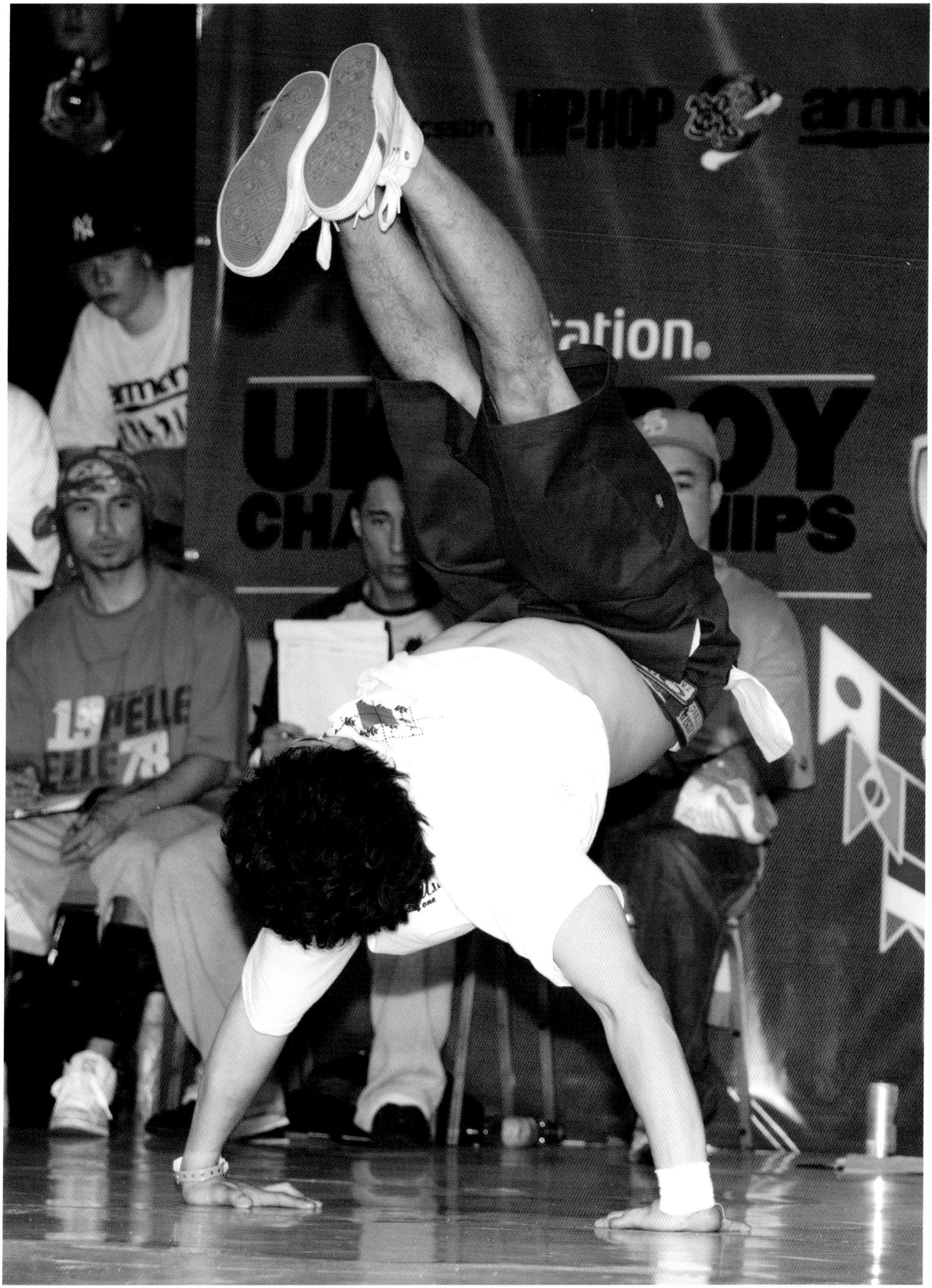
HIP-HOP

DANCERS' STORIES

HONG 10 (HONG YEOUL KIM):

CREW: DRIFTERS & 7 COMANDOZ
WORLD CREW CHAMPION, 2002, 2004, 2005;
CHIEF ROCKA AWARD WINNER 2006

One day when I was a kid, one of my friends danced in front of me. I thought, I could be just as good as him. So I went home and practised on my own. I wasn't that serious about it at first, but that was 13 years ago and I'm still b-boying.

When I was first b-boying, every process was through battling. I would practise with my friends via battle; there was no win or lose back then. The battle between Kyung-sung middle school and Jung Ang middle school is the first battle that I remember. Ki-Hyun was on my team and our opponents were Dong In Shin, Kyung Shik Na and Ho Jin Hwang. They were the best b-boys at the time and we were no match for them, but we became friends afterwards.

At first I just wanted to be good at dancing, and as I got better I had a chance to join the Expression Crew. But after winning the 2002 Battle of the Year and UK B-Boy Championships, I lost interest in b-boying. So I stopped for a while, but when I got back into it, I wanted to b-boy forever. Currently I'm with Dream Drifters and 7 Comandoz Crew. I've gained a lot of experience with Dream Drifters and I plan to achieve bigger things with 7 Comandoz.

I try to practise every day: it's a bit plain compared to cyphering, but I like to practise this way.

For me the technique is the most important aspect of b-boying. But dancing is based on music, which is the essential component of b-boying. Adding our own techniques to this basic dance is how we break dance. Sometimes I like to dance to b-boy music, and sometimes to a slow hip-hop or even to house music.

My first battle at the B-Boy Championships was back in 2002. It was our debut and we won the crew battle, and I came second in solo b-boy. It was the most memorable championship because it was my first time participating in such an event, and I'd never had so much fun. I've learned a lot from that trip. 2009 was also a good experience, even though we lost in the semi-finals, we fought well against the States and it inspired me to do better in the future.

INSPIRATIONS:

Anyone that dances. I like Japanese DJs – DJ Ma, DJ Light, DJ Tee. I often dance to their mix tapes.

DANCERS' STORIES

MORRIS (MORRIS EDWARD ISBY III), USA

CREW: FALLEN KINGS
WORLD SOLO B-BOY CHAMPION 2009

I've been dancing my whole life, but I've been b-boying for 12 years, after seeing some local b-boys dancing at a rally at my high school. I told them it looked easy; they told me to prove it... The rest was magic, ha!

My first battle was at a church jam called Peace To Da Streets in Elk Grove, California, April 2000. It felt amazing: all the rawness and not knowing what other b-boys could do. I had a lot to prove though, so I didn't care: I just wanted to battle. I lost in the second round, but was in the top 32.

Before b-boying, I had no passion for anything other than family. B-boying kept me from getting into a lot of the trouble that my friends and family were involved in at that time. Without it I would be a totally different person.

I'm part of Fallen Kings crew. Having a crew is like having a second family, so you feel that regardless of what happens they will always have your back. And you can get inspiration just from training with them, because we all have different ways of thinking.

I train three times a week – full-out practices. In my opinion I battle some of the elite dancers in the world so I can't just cypher all day and think I'm ready; but cyphering helps get your nerves good before you battle. When I'm old and grey, the Champs will be top of my list of stories to tell!

INSPIRATIONS

Morris Isby I (my gramps!), and my favourite DJs are Renegade, Skeme Richards, Tee, Mista Sweet, Meisa, Ex, Jebel, Panic...

DANCERS' STORIES

JUNIOR (JUNIOR BOSILA BANYA), FRANCE:

CREW: WANTED POSSE CREW
B-BOY

I started dancing in 1995, inspired by video clips of MJ, and also by some friends and family who danced. My first battle was back in 1996 or 1997, and it was amazing to see so many people with the same passion in one place. Everyone was dancing in cyphers and it was the first time I could see so many good moves: I was so excited.

B-boying taught and helped me to fight more in life, to stand up for myself. As part of the Wanted Posse crew, I see lots of different styles of dancing – and each one of them inspires me. And there are certain tracks which really make me go off – Society's 'Yes Indeed', Gang Starr's 'Skills'...

When I am at home I can practise my techniques and moves but with some friends we often do cyphers as well. I can practise most of the week when I have time for myself. I travel a lot to do shows, masterclasses and battles to compete or to judge. I've only been at the Champs once, but I wasn't prepared enough for such a big event, and would love to have another chance there.

For me, to be at the top, you either have to be very good at everything or you have to be the best in your particular style. France are producing the best breakers right now, of course! USA and Korea are amazing but now there are no longer only a few big nations for b-boying; you can find good breakers everywhere.

Junior's amazing upper body strength is his trademark, enabling him to hold insane freezes. He is also the most-watched b-boy on YouTube, with over 50 million views.

Make some noise! Supporting your crew members is what it's all about.

Robin (Russia, Top 9) vs Lilou (France, Pokémon): two huge personalities and phenomenal breakers.

The battle between Lilou and Robin was explosive from the start.

DANCERS' STORIES

LILOU (ALI RAMDANI), FRANCE

CREW: POKEMON
CHIEF ROCKA AWARD WINNER 2005;
WORLD CREW CHAMPION, 2006

I've danced for 14 years now, and have been b-boying since 1997-8. Before that I was dancing, doing some popping and locking. I was just a young kid though, not doing it seriously.

I was inspired to take it up after seeing some b-boys on TV, I don't remember who - and I love extreme sports; when b-boys battle it is like an extreme sport. It's about how to turn, balance, how to use your hands...

My first battle was in 1999, in a small town, and I went with people from my 'hood in a car. I didn't tell my parents I was going! It was two hours by car so I said nothing and just went. I won but I don't remember who it was against - some of the b-boys from Silent Tricks were there. It was their first battle too.

B-boying used to be a hobby, but now, if you count the days I have away from home - travelling, dancing - it's 70-80% of my time.

Being in a crew for me affects my dancing a lot. I wouldn't have got where I am now without being in a crew. We support each other - when you do something right, or do something wrong, they tell you. You don't forget where you're from when you're part of a crew; you support each other when you have to make decisions. They give me advice. They will push me to practise and say if something's good or bad. They are honest - more like family than a crew.

DANCERS' STORIES

MENNO (MENNO VAN GORP), HOLLAND

CREW: HUSTLE KIDZ & DEF DOGZ
SOLO B-BOY CHAMPION 2007

I've been dancing since 2001–2. I was inspired to start breaking by all the people doing it around me in my home city; and particularly my two older cousins. My first battle was nine years ago on the street near where I live – we had a street area vs street area battle. When I started it was just for fun, and I was one of the weakest links, but I felt I wanted to do it more seriously. These days I'm in Hustle Kidz and Def Dogz crews, and they inspire my practice and how I move.

I used to be able to train every day because I'd just left high school and had nothing else to do, but now I'm busy travelling, doing shows, teaching – and what with getting older and having other things in my life, I don't have time for daily practice. However, I keep myself moving all the time; working hard and having fun. When I practise I don't think too much – I just do it.

The tracks that make me go wild are tracks where you can feel something extra – not just the beat from the drums and bongos that you hit. Some songs you have to move wild to, and go all out; some just make you move smooth. Having that musicality is so important. If you are a real b-boy you've got to love everything – the style, power, technique and musicality.

It's hard to say who is producing the best b-boys, but I think the dopest scenes right now are in Europe, USA and Russia/Ukraine.

INSPIRATIONS:

Bob Marley. My favourite DJs are Renegade, Timber, Cut Nice and Mista Sweet.

DANCERS' STORIES

ROXRITE (OMAR O. DELGADO MACIAS), USA

**CREW: RENEGADES AND SQUADRON
SOLO B-BOY CHAMPION, 2005**

I've been dancing for 16 years now. What inspired me to start b-boying was seeing kids at my school doing a show, along with others in my grade breaking as well. I also think it was the connection between the people that did it. They were just like me: Hispanic kids with similar backgrounds.

My first battle happened like a week after I started breakin'. It was a cool experience but also a bit nerve-wracking. No one knew I'd tried to break at the time and one of my friends didn't want to battle this guy who had called him out so I said 'I'll battle him for you'. We ended up battling a few rounds and I just kept thinking 'What am I going to do?' He had been dancing longer than me. I did an air twist to a worm and I think that ended the battle, which is funny because since then I have never used a worm in any other battle.

B-boying has had a huge impact on my life: besides it becoming my job it has moulded me into the person I am today. It has provided a lot of opportunities that I never imagined and given me memories that will last a lifetime. I train every other day, sometimes daily. Now my practices feel more like I'm cyphering. Sometimes you do have to go back to hard sessions of developing moves though. Musically, I go off to rare breaks I don't normally hear at jams.

I am currently representing Renegades and Squadron, though I have affiliations with other crews as well. Being a part of a crew helps you develop your dance and find inspiration. It helps you learn and at the same time teach. To be on top of your game I think you need all elements – musicality, strength and technique – not just one or the other. I think you need to understand how to use traditional movements to make you look more dynamic with your style. Sometimes hiding behind one technique or strength will show your weakness, so you have to expand.

Man, my first time to the UK Champs in 2005 was a memorable and life-changing event for me. I went there hungry, ready to take on the world. This was the event that gave me the opportunity to prove myself on a bigger stage than I was used too. I was shocked to see the amount of people that were there just to watch b-boys battle. It was an incredible experience being there and battling some of the best talent in the world. It was my tenth year in the dance and it was also the UK Champs 10-year anniversary so to claim the title meant a lot!

INSPIRATIONS

My brother and my inspirations in b-boyin': Ken Swift, Remind and Ground Level.

Lilou versus Flying Buddah: Despite taking every other major title, Lilou hasn't triumphed yet in the Solos.

The final battle was a tense affair. Both dancers gave everything but it was Buddah that took the title.

WORLD CREW

FOR MANY, THE WORLD CREW BATTLE IS THE MAIN EVENT OF THE B-BOY CHAMPIONSHIPS. EIGHT CREWS FROM AROUND THE WORLD CARRY WITH THEM THE PRIDE OF THEIR NATIONS, AS THEY SET OUT TO TAKE THE TITLE OF 'WORLD'S BEST CREW'.

Reputations have been made and lost here, so the stakes are always high, which makes the battling intense and truly compelling.

Winning the world's biggest battle is arguably the most coveted achievement for any crew. For some it will only ever be a dream, but make no mistake, every crew comes to win.

Each year the crews get better and better. There can be few spectacles as entertaining as the crew battles at the B-Boy Championships. So get ready to see an explosion of style and power with incredible routines and jaw-dropping moves as they battle it out to become the illest in the game.

Hong10 and Project Soul (Korea) changed the game in 2002, taking the crew title on their first attempt.

This one's for you: B-boy Cloud points to his crew and takes flight during the 2009 final.

Project Drifterz Crew, Korea: Hong 10 and Zero 9 in battle mode, doing a crazy routine in the 2009 crew final.

Jinjo crew (Korea) at full speed.

Classic b-boy style on display in the crew battles: Flea Rock and Luigi, Skill Methodz (USA).

B-boy Abstrak, Methodz of Havic (USA), hittin' beats. His amazing
musicality and supreme flow are on perfect display in the crew battles.

DANCERS' STORIES

TEKNYC (JOEL MARTINEZ), USA

**CREW: SKILLMETHODZ
WORLD CREW CHAMPION, 2003**

I've been dancing all my life but I've only been breaking for 16 years. I've been inspired by different things – my older brother Willy, who in the mid-80s was one of the top b-boys in Puerto Rico inspired me to start dancing, as did the book *Where I was Born & Raised*, the movies *Wild Style*, *Style Wars* and *Beat Street* and later in '96 I saw a group of street performers in Tampa, Florida – 'United Street Artists'.

My first battle was in Tampa against a local crew. It was at a small hip-hop event. It was raw, we were all just catching wreck and vibing. Since then, breaking has changed my life. I've been all over the world and met incredible people. I've been living my dream life. I feel the opportunities I've gotten and the experiences I've had have shaped me into the man I am today.

I am a proud member of the SkillMethodz crew. Being part of a crew affects how you break because you're not only reppin' yourself, you're also reppin' everyone in your crew, and what we all stand for. The pressure is higher, but it's also a great driving force to continue to get better. We feed off each other and push each other to strive to continue to be better day in and day out.

I train about three times a week. Every time you get down and catch wreck is a learning process, especially for those of us who freestyle. There's always something new that we learn, sometimes, some moments, moves and transitions never happen because they're not meant to. They're meant to happen in that moment, to that particular song, in that particular place. You simply gotta carpe diem. There are so many tracks that make me go off, from Apache 'Give It Up, Turn It Lose', ' Breakers' Revenge', 'Don't Sweat the Technique', 'T Plays It Cool'. Oh man! Too many to choose from.

Being at the top of your game is having a healthy combination of technique, musicality and strength, as well as having knowledge of the dance, the culture and its history. Without these key elements you'll never truly excel. In order to be anywhere near the top you first have to know where this dance comes from, who allowed it even to exist in the first place, why it does exist. Then the rest – strength, technicality, musicality, etc. – comes after. I think we are seeing a lot of incredible talent everywhere and that's a positive thing.

UK champs is the goal: it's the jam our generation came up watching on vhs tapes and hoped to one day go to. To have gone and be part of it, dance on that stage and furthermore to win it, what can I say, mission accomplished!

INSPIRATIONS:

James Brown, Muhammad Ali and Roberto Clemente.

FAVOURITE DJS:

Skeme Richards, Unkle Chip, Sickroc, Lean Rock, Basic and Kenny Dope.

Skill Methodz and Havic Koro, USA, came together to form
Methodz of Havic, the taking the World Crew title in 2003.

'Hold up, wait a minute!' Gravity, Dynamic Rockers (USA) showcases his power moves.

Koko from EXG (Holland) hits his aerial spin.

Lu'Chisz of EXG.

Group formation: Dynamic Rockers.

Lean Back: Another memorable Top 9 routine.

B-girl Roxy flips out: Soul Mavericks (UK) in action against Zulu Kingz Worldwide.

DANCERS' STORIES

ROXY (ROXANNE MILLINER), UK

CREW: SOUL MAVERICKS
B-GIRL BATTLE WINNER, 2010

My brother is a stand-up dancer, and when I started dancing almost five years ago I always kinda copied him. But I was a bit too shy to dance, so I started off doing handstands, and someone spotted me and told me to come and train with them at a b-boy spot.

The first battle I did was at Mighty 4 UK b-girl. I didn't sign up for it; I just went to watch, but somebody didn't come when their name was called so I jumped in, and I won! It was the best feeling ever. I was so hyped and loved the music, and I just went off!

B-boying has changed my life. It's made me grow up a lot: I have travelled all around the world, I've learnt to discipline myself, I've met all kinds of different people, danced in front crowds of thousands, been on TV, and I've been introduced to so much music I wouldn't have known about if I wasn't dancing. It has made my life spectacular!

I'm in Soul Mavericks crew. Being part of a crew makes my dancing 100 times better. I learn from them - moves and mentality - we travel together and battle together, and we feed off of each other when we battle, it's dope!

I personally prefer someone to have more musicality, than technique and strength, but the best b-boys/b-girls have it all.

Girls are getting better now, but still most b-girls get easy props when they don't deserve it.

There's no need, b-girls can be just as good as b-boys. USA are the most consistent in always having dope b-boys, and there are a lot of crazy European b-boys making noise now, but Japan have the best b-girls.

I go to practice sessions as much as I can, mostly to learn moves. I don't train every day but most days I dance in shows or at clubs. When I battle and go to clubs, that's when I'm improving my dancing. I love it when I'm in a battle and I hear a dope, hyped track that I've never heard before.

I have battled at the Champs in the crews three times, we got to the semi-finals in 2010, and the 3on3 b-girl battle twice, we got to the finals in 2009, and won in 2010. It is one of, if not the best jams in the world, in my opinion. The amount of amazing b-boys, b-girls, poppers and lockers that come to compete and watch from all over the world gives it such a good vibe. It's competitive, but not intimidating. The first day of Champs has so much going on; the cyphers are always on fire, the battles are always full of dope b-boys and b-girls. Then the finals on day two is just insane! The DJs are always the best, and it has all of the best b-boys in the world competing. The crowd is so huge, it gives you such a buzz when you are on stage. Even before I competed, just watching the Champs blew my mind ... and the afterparty is always dope!

INSPIRATIONS

James Brown, and Junior from Wanted Posse was my first inspiration, AMAZING moves and really humble!

B-boy Mounir (France), Vagabond crew, 'sticks' his freeze perfectly.

Prepare to launch: one of the Vagabond crew's endless supply of dope routines.

Above: Vagabonds of France vs Amazon b-boys (Brazil), 2010. *Opposite:* Brazilian b-boy flies.

Spee-D and Flipz, Endangered Species/Skill Methodz (USA) all-star crew, flip in synch.

Cloud's unique style and character has made him one of the superstars in the game.

DANCERS' STORIES

VENUM (JAIME BURGOS III):

CREW: SKILLMETHODZ
WORLD CREW CHAMPION, 2009

I have been engulfed in breakin' since the very first day I was introduced to it. I was invited to the club one night by my boy Benji and his cousin. Truthfully, I only had five dollars to my name at the time and it cost exactly five dollars to get in. I had already planned on going and spending the evening outside the club, just hanging out, but the combination of my boredom and the hype music blaring through the club doors was enough to lure me in and convince me to part ways with my last five.

For the first time in my life I saw b-boys in a cypher and was immediately hypnotised by their fluid, acrobatic movements. Being a street tumbler, I felt an immediate connection, and knew that I could and had to do this. I truly believe that our passions choose us; we don't choose them. I found my calling, and that is how five dollars changed my life.

My first battle was at that very same club two weeks after my first breakin' encounter. I was so eager and excited to learn that I had Benji start training me the very next day. I didn't really know what I was doing; I just combined my flips with the moves Benji taught me and threw myself into the cypher without a care in the world. I was so happy to be dancing that onlookers' opinions and judgements were irrelevant and nonexistent in my world. It was the most amazing experience and just the beginning of the journey I was about to embark on.

I am who I am today because of this dance. It has moulded me into a strong, successful and confident individual through artistic growth and creative development. It has allowed me to open my mind in ways I never thought possible while teaching me how to bring out my best qualities as a dancer and human being.

I am an original member of the Skillz Methods Crew along with Cloud, Abstract, Flipz... We are some of the best and most innovative at what we do in the world, and we are that way because of each other. We believe in each other's talents and constantly push each other to grow and get better. Having a crew gives you a sense of brotherhood and support that you'd never have solo. Through them I've been given a sense of family and support that I'd never experienced before. My real family was broken. My father was in prison, and my brother was also in and out of jail. I was surrounded by so much negativity – drugs, prostitution, theft – it would have been easy for me to continue to go down the wrong path. I had already been arrested several times for underage drinking and breaking into a car, and I knew I wanted more for myself and my future, so I enrolled in a program called 'Job Core', which was designed to give youths the proper skills to be successful in life. But it was truly breakin' that saved my life: it gave me hope, freedom and ambition; it inspired me to dream big and gave me the courage to make my dream a reality. I am blessed with the opportunities to travel and make a living doing what I love while being in a place that I am able to give back to my community.

I'd say when I'm with my crew I cypher about 80% of the time, but cyphering only improves my musicality and freestyle ability. The rest is repetition and dedication; there are hours of hard work that go into mastering a move. You must

work that go into mastering a move. You must have heart, dedication and the desire to achieve and never give up. With that said, I don't train every day because I believe it is important to have balance. Especially, because I have a son and I want to be sure that I give him the time he deserves too. Even without a child I feel that training every day will put too much strain on the mind and body. Balance is key in all aspects of life.

As a b-boy, everything should be done in connection to the music. Give me James Brown and I feel funky, throw on some Rakim and I wanna get rugged and explosive. I don't think technique, strength and musicality should be viewed as separate entities in relation to dance. Neither is more important than the other because they work synergistically to create the pictures in your movement. In order to be at the top of the game I feel every b-boy should be fluent in all three of these essential elements. Furthermore, you must have endurance not only in your body, but in your mind as well.

The UK Champs have been amazing because as a competitor you go up against some of the top crews around the world. It is a platform for b-boys/b-girls to share our art and being there exposes us to all the eccentric styles each country has to offer. It's so dope to be in a place where so many people share the same love for hip-hop culture.

INSPIRATIONS:

There are so many. I greatly admire and respect all the underdogs who came from nothing and had the tenacity to pursue their heart's desires regardless of the hardships that faced them; those that dreamed the impossible. People like Bruce Lee and Mike Tyson who beat the odds of their upbringing. I would also want to meet Einstein because to me he was out of his mind! He gave his brilliance and wisdom to the world by sharing theories and innovations way ahead of his time despite the scrutiny of cynics. And I'd like to dedicate this piece to my son Alejandro Burgosm who is my biggest inspiration in life. No matter how hard things get in life, never give up on your dreams.

Pokémon in battle in 2006 (*above*) and 2007 (*right*). Lilou, Brahim and co. have grown up battling at the Champs, becoming the World Crew Champions in 2006 on their third attempt.

T.I.P. (Korea) winning the crew final against Top 9 of Russia. *Right*: B-boy Snake of T.I.P. rocking upside down.

WHAT THE JUDGES ARE LOOKING FOR...

STORM

Judging criteria (B-Boying, Popping, Locking):

a) Dynamics, which is the symbiosis of musicality, the energy, or explosiveness, spontaneity, timing and dramaturgy.

b) Dimension, which is the symbiosis of the body composition, spatial awareness and the use of all possible levels. Both criteria are filtered through control. Which shows how steady you are.

c) Character, which is mainly looked at as stage presence, but also looked at in character moves like gestures and miming.

SALAH

Judging criteria (Popping):

When I'm judging, I am looking at the moment. If I know the dancer I will judge him for what he is doing that day, there and then; I will not judge him like the fact I know he danced better previously. Judges have to focus on the present not the past. I look for who controls the battle, who is more technical, who will be smart and use the musicality, who will do a move I will never forget, who will be creative.... These are what I look for.

Tough call: Every time I judge I take my pen and paper, then when I watch the dancer I make notes, score points, and when the battle finishes I look at my paper and see who has the best score. It's more easy for me that way, though not always! This is why organisers have to choose judges with experience, not a 'name' dancer... Winning a battle doesn't mean you can be a judge; you need to have a lot of experience for that. Your biography will tell you if you can be judge or not.

GEMINI

Judging criteria (Locking):

I've been in an organised battle before, so I know how you feel when you are in it. So I am trying to analyse the battle as best I can. I take notes if I need to, and respect everyone who enters the contest. Then, basically, I am looking mostly at who will meld most with the music, and show knowledge of the dance style and originality, groove and technique, rhythm and battle skills. It's a locking 'battle' not a showcase or a party. Personally I think in the locking scene some people are entering and don't really understand where they are at, which can create some confusion.

Tough call: I do my best to keep my focus during the entire battle, and judge the moment. If, after all my 'battle criteria', I can't decide, then my personal taste will make my decision - sometimes the crowd or other judges might feel differently, but you've gotta do your job and make your own decision.

LAMINE

Judging criteria (B-boying):

I judge the musicality and the cleanness first, then originality.

Tough call: I take my responsibilities as a judge seriously and am always ready to defend my decisions.

CROS1

Judging criteria (B-Boying):

I look for the complete package: from dancing into and out of the cypher, to throwing down some ill footwork, flowing, freezes, power moves, tricks - it's like the b-boys are telling a story from beginning to end.

Tough call: It can get pretty intense sometimes but at the end of the day you gotta know that regardless there's only one winner and one loser; you can't please everyone. I just try to keep track of the rounds as best as I possibly can, so at the end of the battle I can see who won the most rounds to come out victorious. So to those b-boys out there reading this, don't give up any rounds!!

J SMOOTH

Judging criteria (Popping):

I'm looking for poppin', freedom, energy and battle ability - ie, if the person is really battling, either looking at the opponent and making eye contact, like he's saying 'Watch - this is how you do it' or by getting up in his face. I need to see a battle, not just getting down.

Tough call: I go with my first instinct always. I trust in my first reaction. I don't ever want to second guess myself.

THE HOST'S STORY

AFRIKA ISLAM, USA

In a place called the Bronx, in a city called New York, in the ghetto of a melting pot of musical fusion, low income and high hopes, beans and rice, patties and projects, street gangs and drugs... something great happened. The beat, the dance, the battle: b-boy was born. It was a time of freedom, no limits, no excuses, no awards. Just bring it and bring it hard. Today you win, tomorrow you defend your title again.

I was a member of the Zulu Kings. The b-boys that represented the young new Zulu nation. My job was to dance, search out, destroy, crush 'em, battle... Then after that was done, hear the music and express myself in the way of peace. I was a dance warrior. My style was speed and moves. F*** the rest. Zulu Kings lived to be the best.

I'm known as the son of Afrika Bambaataa for a reason, but I was a student of both Grand Master Flash and Afrika Bambaataa as well as Kool Herc, the hip-hop of day one. I arrived day one.

The jams were in schools, in the basketball courts, at the parks, in the back of buildings, in the streets in the summer heat, and in every boom box that had a beat. Freedom to express your way of what is now called hip-hop. To us it was just us. Our way of the street warrior. Parties in the park, Converse, Puma, PF flyers, t-shirts, tank tops, low-to-no money, girls, gangsters, dealers, players and music. Not any music; our music.

I produced a lot of things: the first hip-hop radio show, Zulu beats... I got into it as leader of my first group, The Funk Machine, with Donald D and L Jay, Kid Vicious, Busy Bee, Melle Mel, Grand Master Caz, Ice-T... I think I was always a producer; ever since I did my first pause tape. I made fusion beats in my bedroom – after school. Classic.

B-boy is the true art form. Skills and determination. It's always the same. The b-boys change but the competition stays the same. Two men enter, one man leaves with his hand raised, as the champ. That's what I think: come hard, or don't come at all. B-boy lives no matter what.

Truth is the god of b-boys – it sent me an SMS. I was on Planet X at an alien sex bar. The message said 'You're needed' so I got on my ship and beamed down to see the new generation get down, round by round to the crown. B-boy Champs don't f*** around.

There are too many *America's Got Talent* bulls*** shows made on the backs of b-boys and girls. Street dance taught in the dance classes of the rich, taken from the true school and put on pop culture, TV. Wackass Timberfake and Husher, Lady Goon Ga and Justin Bean Head. Nuff said.

The future is unwritten, but the writers are many and the army is strong and the real is real is back by tradition, blood, sweat and fears. Come October every year you will see the future and it is called Battle UK B-Boy champs. Don't get me started, Homie.

JUDGES' STORIES

TUF TIM TWIST, UK

CREW: ROCK STEADY CREW
SOLO B-BOY CHAMPION, 1999

I have danced since I was young – I was into punk and ska and also danced Northern Soul – but started b-boying in late 1983. I grew up on American culture; TV shows, cartoons and comic books, so I loved anything American.

I was dancing Northern Soul at the time hip-hop came over to the UK from NYC. As soon as I saw breaking I knew it was for me. It was like an advanced, futuristic style of Northern Soul. People don't realise the similarity between the two dances: we danced on top, we had spins, drops and acrobatics; but one thing that stands out to me was how we had particular parts of the records when we waited to execute the drops and moves, just like the drum break in breaking. So it was the challenge of a new dance that attracted me, and the freedom to be original and create new moves.

Back in the early years we always battled as a crew. The first real significant battle I had was with my crew, Magic Force, and it was in Glasgow against the Glasgow City Breakers in 1985. It was at a street festival on the riverside in Glasgow on a big stage, and was a tuf battle.

Being in a crew is what it's all about for me. I'm a member of Rock Steady Crew. Crew should be like family: it reflects life itself, with a lot of ups and downs. Life ain't easy, but love and respect is very important. B-boying is my life; hip-hop is my life. It's been a real rollercoaster ride around the world. Dope b-boys/girls are popping up everywhere these days. Every corner of the planet have dope styles and that's gotta be good for the culture.

Over the years, with age and injuries, my training has changed, but if I could I would dance all day, every day. Back in the beginning I used to train up to eight hours a day... If you're new to b-boying, or young, you should be doing as much as possible. To be an all-round b-boy you gotta have as much as possible to beat the best. I never tell someone to take away – just keep adding. I would love to meet me back in 1983 and tell myself to train harder and believe in yourself more, and prepare for your future.

While I don't have a track I can say is 'the one' for me to b-boy to, the classics still do it for me: 'The Mexican', 'Apache', and James Brown all day...

Seeing the Champs grow over the years has been amazing. I have seen the ins and outs of the event. It's not easy putting it together each year and I've got nothing but love and respect for Hooch for doing it and hanging in when it's tuf. Being a solo winner in 1999 is still a great achievement for me. Seeing Crazy Legs and Babe Ruth rock together on the stage at Brixton; that was hip-hop history. Seeing DJ Leacy rock the Champs... an honour. And to be able to watch the continued progression of the b-boy culture at the Champs is beautiful. Peace and love to the world of b-boying.

FAVOURITE DJ:

DJ Leacy. Rest in peace brotha...

CROS1 (CHRIS WRIGHT), USA
CREW: ARMORY MASSIVE; B-BOY

In the 80s breaking was the thing to do. I dabbled a bit in 84-85 when EVERYONE was doing it, then stopped like everyone else when it died out. In the 90s I started again because I still missed the days of breaking, and when I saw other people doing it again I was like, YES!! It was a release for me to get all my cares and worries out through my dancing. I haven't been dancing much for the past years due to some injuries but I'm still a b-boy at heart.

B-boying has not only impacted my life, it is my life. It made me who I am and it's my business, so it's everything I've revolved myself around. Even when I'm doing things that have nothing to do with b-boying I attack it like a b-boy!

My first battle was at my neighbour's house in 84. It was intense because all the neighbours were there cyphering in my friend's back yard. I got a crazy rush.

Armory Massive, my crew, is more of a hip-hop conglomerate; a group of like-minded individuals from all over the world. Your crew hold you down and you do the same for them. It gives you added fuel for your fire.

You've got to have everything to be on top in breaking. The music is producing the best breakers. Those that listen to the music will make their way to the top. For me James Brown records are a sure shot!

I've been a judge for the past six years now and it's always been good. I always look forward to seeing the dope b-boys from around the world, and of course the after parties with all my friends - new and old. The weekend is solid from beginning to end.

JUDGES' STORIES

STORM (NIELS ROBITZKY), GERMANY:

CREW: BATTLE SQUAD, ANIMATRONIK
B-BOY AND POPPER

I've danced all my life, but got into b-boying and popping in the summer of 1983. As a kid I created a little dream world through cartoons and superhero comics: when I saw b-boying and popping I realised I could make that dream world a reality.

Hip-hop seriously saved me. I grew up in north Germany, and my parents were part of a generation that had witnessed war. We were the first generation that really had to question our forefathers and their morals and beliefs. We learned that Germany had really messed up, and some Germans had been probably the worst kind of people on the entire planet. At the same time we knew that we didn't have anything to do with it and that nobody could blame us.

Basically, we all grew up searching for an identity. I realised pretty fast that I actually came from Planet Hip-Hop. I was always creative and loved music and art. Dancing became my passion and an escape from all the BS out there; that's how it is still. But at the same time, it was the best therapy in life as well. The social aspect of dance especially made me learn more than anything. I used dance to communicate, more than my mouth.

I'm part of two crews. One is the legendary 'Battle Squad', who won the Battle of the Year (BOTY) twice, and means a lot to me, because we grew up together as people and not just as dancers. Our goal was never to win as many battles as possible. We always looked at each other much more as artists and we knew that if we grew too far away from the original b-boy format, we might get misunderstood.

The other crew, Animatronik, is a science- and dance-based crew that was created in 2005. We love the art of popping and everything that falls under that umbrella name. From diagnosing why we do this dance, to the architecture of the counter move, in this group we practise, test, analyse and theorize in a very academic manner. Our work field is not just dance floors, studios and practice rooms, but also studies in fields that are not so related on first thought. From computer programs that can test the intensity of your pop, to studies in NLP and philosophy, we'll incorporate anything that could improve the texture of our dance culture.

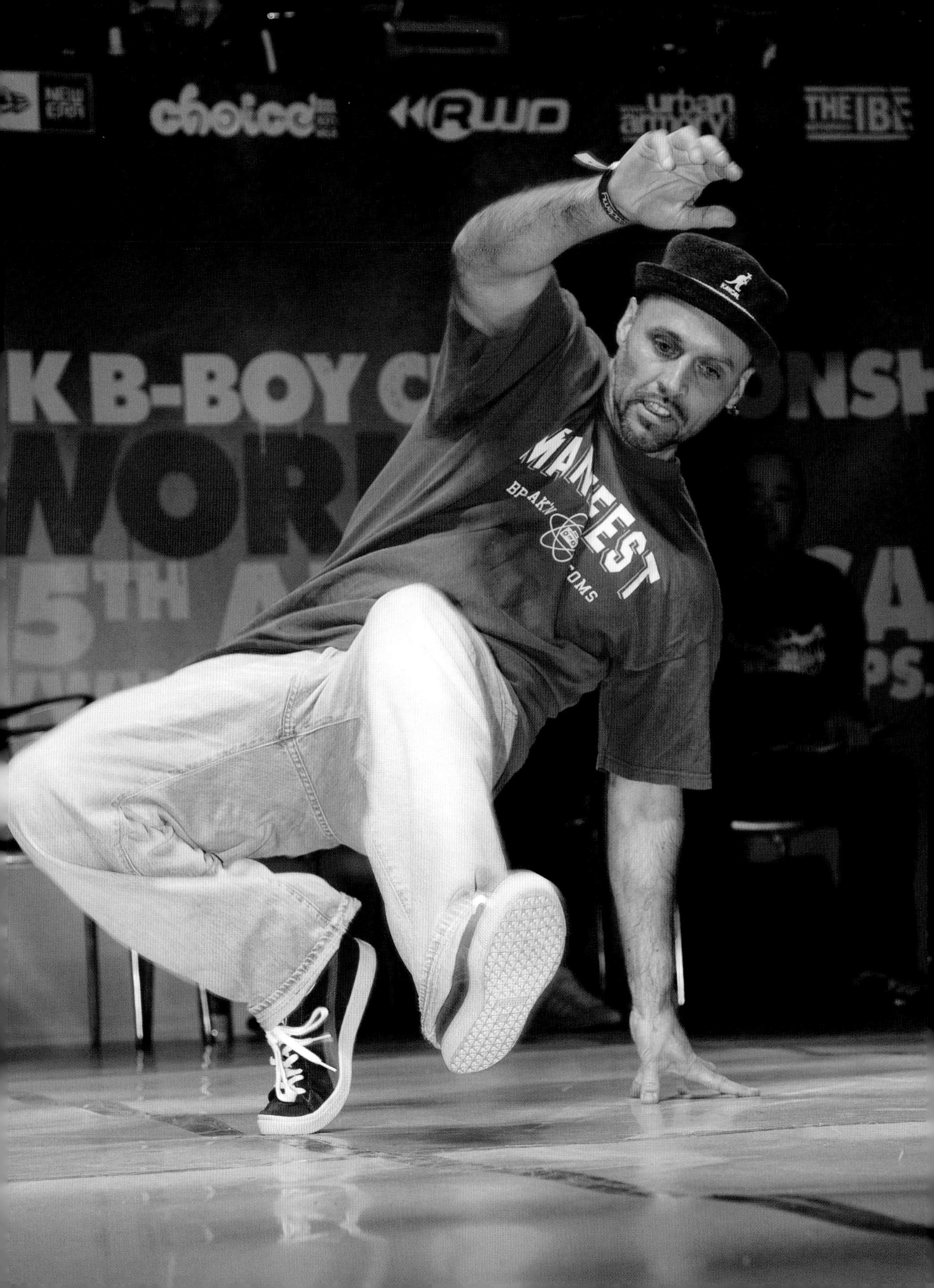

choice
RWD
urban armory
K B-BOY C
ONSH
5TH

JUDGES' STORIES

LAMINE (LAMINE DIOUF), FRANCE:

CREW: CO-FOUNDER OF VAGABONDS B-BOY

I've been dancing since 1991. I had a lot of problems when I was young, and b-boying helped me get back on track. I was inspired by a crew called Fantastic Four from my neighbourhood, and then by PCB9 (Paris City Breakers), Aktuel Force and The Family.

My first battle was against a neighbourhood crew that is well-known today: Wanted Posse. We were mates, but when we battled we were enemies: that didn't hinder the respect, however, which is the very essence of battles.

I don't have a crew now, but I'm the co-founder of the legendary crew Vagabonds. It was a great experience being a part of it, and we were like family. We got together in a flat at about midday, went for lunch, then trained together, had more food at 7pm, then went on for more training, ate at midnight, then headed on to train in Parisian clubs before going to sleep – this went on for about six years! I still train every day, or at least I try to. My favourite track to go off on is The Electric Light Orchestra 'Fire on High'.

You need to be an all-round dancer today. All breakers are different, and I think the most important thing to stand out is that: be original.

JUDGES' STORIES

GEMINI (FABRICE ARAGONES), FRANCE:

LOCKER; FOUNDER OF LOCKING4LIFE

I started dancing around 1989 after meeting some guys in my neighbourhood who were really into dancing, and – if I'm honest – saw the impact dancing had on girls! Then later on I fell in love with the whole culture; the music, the graffiti, the fashion... The whole package was so powerful – I just loved it all.

The first dancers I hung out with were very competitive, and my first teacher used to train us in a battle environment all the time and I wanted to prove to myself that I could make it. So my first battles were with my crew members, and the people who used to practise at the same places as us; then later on, we started to go to clubs in Paris with a strong battle attitude.

Locking totally changed my life. Before it I was into bikes and football, and was also a really good student in school. My parents wanted me to have a good education and pursue a 'real job', but I was not motivated by anything other than dancing. When I tried to explain the situation to my parents, they didn't like it – especially my dad. He said 'What? You wanna be a professional dancer?' It was very hard in the beginning. I feel really lucky that my parents trusted me later on – though of course I really had to prove myself to them.

I've been part of a few crews, but now I am solo, hanging out with a lot of crews and dancers from all around the world. Recently I developed a concept that became an international movement, called Locking4Life. It's not a crew - more an idea, a vision, of the Locking dance style. If you share the Locking4Life ideas you are free to join: the main motto is 'Respect the past. Live the present. Build the Future.'

I am really into 90s hip-hop, New Jack Swing – probably because I started around that time, and it makes me feel great any time I hear classics of that period. Then of course soul, funk and R'n'B. I am trying to listen to anything that inspires me; it can be any kind of music.

I used to train every day in my early years, now, I am cyphering or do some sessions with some friends in my home or at some practice spots, when I am feeling it. Some dancers come from a 'technical aspect', others from a 'feeling aspect'; it depends on your cultural experiences, your personality. I think the best thing is to be balanced and comfortable in both aspects, and on top of that you need to keep the love and the passion for what you do.

All around the world you can find some really good lockers, but for me Asian countries are where you will find the strongest Locking scene. Asian countries are more into it than the rest of the world, but there are still some really good Lockers coming up from different parts of the globe.

The UK Champs is one of the greatest events in the world: I love it, and to me the Champs organisation is family. I've been working with them for several years now, and it's always been a pleasure. Besides the Locking I also love to watch those crazy b-boying and popping battles, the atmosphere is great, they are keeping it real, and to me it's an annual rendezvous!
Peace, G. Locking4Life.

THE MUSIC

THE MUSIC

IT WAS A DJ WHO NAMED THE DANCE B-BOYING – THE JAMAICAN-BORN KOOL HERC – AND RIGHT FROM ITS BEGINNINGS TO TODAY, THE DJS ARE CENTRAL TO THE DANCE FORM OF B-BOYING. THE DJS FIRE THE BATTLES: IF THEY PLAY A FLAT SELECTION OF MUSIC, IT'S GOING TO BE A FLAT BATTLE. IT'S UP TO THE DJS TO FIND THE EXCLUSIVE BREAKS IN THE MUSIC FOR THE DANCERS TO 'GO OFF' TO – WHETHER IT'S DRUM BEAT, VOCAL HOOK OR HORN LICK.

As the b-boys go into a battle, they don't know what tracks the DJ is going to play – the point is to react to the music and interpret it; not just the beat and the melody but – with the best dancers – even the scratches the DJ adds in.

As a DJ myself, my introduction to b-boying in the 80s was through music – particularly Malcolm McClaren and the world-famous Supreme Team's song, 'Buffalo Gals', which featured the Rock Steady crew in the video. I was playing reggae and soul at the time, trying to emulate the local Sound Systems that were our inspiration. Sounds like Mastermind, Java Hi-Power, Rap Attack and Saxon, but I had already started playing electro records, which was what hip-hop was called at the time. When tracks like 'Planet Rock' by Afrika Bambaataa and the Extra T's 'ET Boogie' hit the parties it changed everything; and as soon as

the b-boys started throwing down, the first wave truly started.

At the Funkin' Pussy club nights we were playing James Brown, Kool & the Gang, Bar-Kays, The Meters, George Clinton and Bootsy Collins; plus the P-Funk-infused G-Funk tracks exploding out of the west coast like Dr Dre, Snoop Dogg, DJ Quick and Boo-Yaa T.R.I.B.E, and all the great East Coast hip-hop from that 'golden period' of the early to mid-nineties. We had amazing improptu guests come through at the club, including George Clinton and Afrika Islam and Melle Mel.

At the Championships themselves we always have legendary DJs, including Afrika Bambaataa, DJ Renegade, Skeme Richards, Shortee Blitz, the late DJ Leacy...

DJ STORY

DJ LEACY

The DJ and the dancer always ran together in hip-hop; both outdoing contenders simultaneously: the man behind the wheels and the kid in the circle driving each other's expression to the morning.

Holding down this legacy since the mid-80s, DJ 'Leacy' dominated the b-boy sound systems worldwide. Under the influence of break beats and the New York park jams, Leacy was the heart and soul of the party, while the b-boys pioneered their new moves.

Recognised for his rare archive selection and trademark 'doubles', Leacy's numerous performances and mix-tapes made his sought-after records into classics. Whether headlining the UK B-Boy Championships, battle of the Year, B-Boy Pro-AM or the B-Boy Summit, every year he inspired the next generation of music lovers, break fiends and b-boys to ask the same question: 'What is the beat?'

To be called a pioneer in the world of hip-hop is praise indeed, but for James 'Break DJ' Leacy the cap fits. Leacy passed away in 2004 just three weeks after cementing his position as the leading exponent in his field as resident DJ at the 2004 UK B-Boy Championships World Finals.

His sets of raw b-boy breaks, played, cut and scratched back to back were his passion. Leacy's mix-tapes and compilations are still the must-have soundtracks for b-boys, b-girls and music fans across the world.

In his honour, each year the B-Boy Championships present the DJ Leacy 'Chief Rocka' award. This is for the b-boy who rocks hardest to the music in the crew battles. It honours the unique relationships between the true b-boy and the DJ rockin' the beats on the ones and twos. The award is presented as a bespoke graffitied jacket, painted by his close friend, Tim Twist, each year. The jackets, which are works of art in their own right, are cherished and worn with pride by the winning b-boys.

Along with our central banner, painted by Dan Duce and East 3, we keep Leacy front, centre and in the heart of the b-boy circle at the B-boy Championships. Rest in beats break DJ Leacy.

DJ STORY

SKEME RICHARDS, USA
ROCK STEADY CREW/SESSION 31

DJing was something that just called my name artistically. There weren't a lot of people at that time in my neighborhood doing it, and most of those who were were older cats. I started in 1981, but didn't get my own turntables until 1982. I'd always been into 'cool' and unique things growing up, so this was something that had me written all over it. I had already been into writing graffiti, so this being a part of the culture made me want to do it even more.

I remember DJing my first battle like it just happened yesterday! I had just moved to the neighborhood, and the kids I was hanging out with all had older brothers, whose equipment they'd use after school. I tried it, and thought that I was getting pretty good at it, so when the summer time came around we set the equipment up in the back of the house. I called this guy out who I really didn't like: needless to say he smashed me. After that day I said it would never happen again so I practised hard all summer long. Close to the end of summer, we had another battle. The outcome was a lot different this time. I had speed, skills, tricks and better records. I've never lost or let anyone show me up since then!

In the last decade I've been introduced to new genres and re-introduced to old genres that I've grown to appreciate. I try to keep that same attitude that I had when I started, and keep applying it to every generation that goes by so that I stay relevant. Philly has a deep musical history and background. One of the greatest record labels is from my city, Philadelphia International Records, which was known for putting out so much great music. The Jackson 5 recorded some of their best music in Philly. We had a heavy soul scene, and even Doo Wop, so music is in the water! People dance here, even if you look at old episodes of Soul Train, they're doing the Philly Dog and other dances. I'm a heavy Funk 45 collector and a lot of the music on them are prime picking for b-boys and b-girls, and at the time no other DJ was spinning that type of stuff; most were focused on traditional drum breaks.

Anyone who knows about hip-hop knows that it's all about originality, so that's what I had to do to separate myself the rest; I had to break records that no one had heard or been known to spin or break to.

INSPIRATIONS:

legendary graffit artist Dondi White, the Style Master General. This guy was super creative and ahead of his time. His work and attitude inspires me when I DJ and do production.

FAVOURITE TRACKS:

There are so many to choose from, but I love the classics like Incredible Bongo Band's 'Apache', Liquid Liquid's 'Cavern' and Gaz's 'Sing Sing'... I also love the new funky tracks that groups like Budos Band, UK's Funkshone and Ill Boogs put out.

FAVOURITE DJS:

DJ Groove, Grand Master Flash, Jazzy Jeff and Cash Money, Cut Chemist, Shadow, Nu-Mark and the Beat Junkies, King of Diggin, DJ Muro from Japan.

DJ STORY

RENEGADE, UK
SOUL MAVERICKS/RENEGADE'S CREW

Hip-hop changed the idea I had of my life. My uncle was a physicist and that's what I wanted to be – I was all set for NASA! Hip-hop ruined it! When you're young you don't know what's going to happen. I'd been into dance since I was a kid, but I've been in to hip-hop dance since 1982. I'm from South America so we'd have birthday or family parties and everyone would dance – but not breaking.

In 1982 I got exposed to Rock Steady Crew – Malcolm McClaren and that early wave on TV. Everyone from that time has the same references – a few seconds of clips here, a few seconds there. Now there's so much information you could easily miss a YouTube clip – unless it goes viral and everyone's heard about it. Then there were only three TV channels, and if you missed stuff, someone at school had seen it. The whole world was innocent to everything. Someone with white gloves doing the windmill seemed amazing. If you see something like freerunning now, you can relate it to other extreme sports or arts – but when you'd never seen graffiti, or never seen someone spinning around on the floor, it seemed really weird. What was related to? Nothing I knew!

By 1986 that wave of b-boying was dead, and we were the last ones going in London; which was when I got into DJing. While I was at college I met Blade – a hip-hop MC from London, and became his DJ. Within a year or so I was scratching on records. The same crowd of people who were into b-boying came along. When I started out I was DJing for dancers, and when we were touring Europe we met the b-boy crews like Battle Squad and Born to Rock... So my interest in b-boy was still being fed. The English hip-hop sound was big in Europe but not over here. In Germany they were still breaking, so they appreciated what we were doing. The b-boy influence stayed through the music and influenced the next generation of dancers in Europe.

Since the beginning I could see that b-boy was a broad thing – if you want to be a b-boy like Chico with power moves, you have to train like an athlete, or if you're musical dancer then you have a different thing. Competition is what drives the culture and without battling b-boy is dead as a doornail! For me the Champs are like having a nephew – I give input. It's ended up being one of the biggest events in the world, from being a small event in Shepherd's Bush Empire, because it's not afraid to change. It's the place that you see upcoming dancers for the first time; hear great new tracks for the first time.

INSPIRATIONS:

Crazy Legs, Kevin Smith, Popping Pete.

FAVOURITE TRACKS:

Breaking music and popping music is dope – I can do more stuff physically with breaking music but creatively you can do more with popping. I'm a traditionalist; my taste is beats that make me want to break – things that are percussive; not horns and stuff, but beats. At heart I'm a power mover, that's what I liked as a kid. Originally I wanted to do windmills and swipes and turtles. So my breaks are to inspire the big moves as well.

DJ STORY

SHORTEE BLITZ, UK
EXTENDED PLAYERS/KISS FM

I always bought records from when I was a kid, with paper-round money, so I kinda fell into it because I had the music. But the main influences are Cash Money and Jazzy Jeff. These guys have kept it consistently clean since the 80s and they're still doing it year round. Legends.

I've been DJing for 18 years - I don't battle, I just spin... I like it when parties are hype, so I try and get it to that level every time, no matter what music I'm playing. It's all tied together hip-hop wise, 'cause that's me.

Music changes through time, but it goes in cycles. A lot more technology has been introduced, ie serato, which made it easier for the travelling DJ. And you can still rock it with Vinyl.

The fast scratching and cutting I do just came about from trying to keep it interesting. As a busy DJ sometimes you hear tunes thousands of times, so I try to double up, blend, and keep it as neat and fresh as possible. There's definitely an art to DJing. It's always evolving, but the core elements are still there, because it's still relevant. I believe it's not what you play but the way you play it.

There are too many great tracks and records to single out a favourite, but 'Shaft in Africa', 'The Grunt', LTD's 'Love to World' and 'Give it Up or Turn it Loose' spring to mind.

I love that at the B-Boy Champs all the elements are being celebrated. Events like this need to take place; it's important for the culture. It's healthy, and people want to witness these events. Every year, thousands come from all over the world to be a part of this cultural celebration. It's good to be with like-minded people from the world over. It has some of the illest battles and legends in the building. It's an honour to be a part of it.

INSPIRATIONS:

Michael Jackson, James Brown, Isaac Hayes, Barry White, Marvin Gaye... Any of those would suffice!

FAVOURITE DJS:

Premo, Kid Capri, Jazzy Jeff, Cash Money, Extended Players.

UNITED NATIONS OF B-BOYING

UNITED NATIONS OF B-BOYING

THE INTERNATIONAL SPREAD OF BREAKING SHOWS NO SIGN OF SLOWING. IN COUNTRIES ACROSS THE WORLD THERE IS AN EMERGING GENERATION OF B-BOYS AND GIRLS SETTING HIGHER AND HIGHER STANDARDS. THESE ARE SOME OF THE NATIONS TO HAVE COMPETED AT THE B-BOY CHAMPS.

FRANCE

FRANCE HAS BROUGHT US SOME OF THE ALL-TIME GREAT CREWS – PARIS CITY BREAKERS, AKTUEL FORCE, THE FAMILY – AND NOW POKEMON AND VAGABOND CREW, WINNERS OF THE 2010 CREW BATTLE AT THE CHAMPIONSHIPS.

They have some of the most stylish dancers representing them, including Beebish, Lilou, Lamine, Mounir and Salah.

JAPAN

JAPAN HAS A HUGE B-BOY SCENE – THERE'S EVEN A FAMOUS ALL-NIGHT TRAINING SPOT BENEATH AN OFFICE BLOCK IN THE CENTRE OF TOKYO TO ACCOMMODATE THE NATION'S OBSESSION.

There are hundreds of crews competing in the Japanese championships – it needs a series of qualifying events to cope with the numbers of crews and individual dancers aiming for a place at the World Finals in London. Spartanic Rockers brought them to glory in 1998, and with dancers like Wing Zero and K-Tan in Found Nation, the scene shows no sign of fading.

KOREA
WITH LEGENDARY B-BOYS LIKE HONG 10 AND PHYSICX, AND CREWS LIKE DRIFTERZ, PROJECT SOUL, RIVERS AND T.I.P., KOREA IS A B-BOY WORLD-BEATING FORCE.

They've won more crew battles than any other country at the Champs, and are crowd favourites due to their attitude and entertaining style.

UK

IN THE EARLY YEARS OF THE COMPETITION, SECOND TO NONE WERE THE CREW TO BEAT. IN RECENT YEARS THE UK HAS COME STORMING BACK INTO THE B-BOY ELITE, THANKS IN NO SMALL PART TO LONDON'S SOUL MAVERICKS CREW; COMING THROUGH THE RANKS, THEY'VE PROVED THEY HAVE WHAT IT TAKES TO TAKE ON THE WORLD'S BEST AND WIN.

DJ RENEGADE ON SOUL MAVERICKS:

With the help of B-Boy Mouse, Soul Mavericks was created in 2005 to fill the void in the UK and put us back on the map.

Whether people remember it or not, I remember a time before Soul Mavericks and what the dancing was like in the UK. So after we started doing new stuff of course others resisted it, but we'd left old moves behind; for example, no one touched swirls and halos and variations before Yu Jin. When people see someone like that doing a move and think they can do it, it inspires them.

I'm not the best b-boy but I'm producing the best b-boys! Even though they are 3 times National Champs, the crew still ask my advice because I travel a lot and have access to more information. It's like bringing up kids, even when they've left home you still look after them.

RUSSIA

TOP 9 GAVE RUSSIA ITS FIRST CHAMPIONSHIPS' CREW TITLE IN 2008, AND ARE NOW PART ONE OF THE WORLD'S ELITE CREWS.

Robin and Komar are just two of the b-boys showing what an electric scene Russia has, and with Top 9 pushing Vagabonds hard in the final in 2010 you can be sure Russia will be fighting to be crowned the best in the world, year in, year out.

USA

WITH A HISTORY THAT INCLUDES B-BOY ICONS, ROCK STEADY CREW, PLUS LEGENDARY CREWS BATTLING AT THE CHAMPS INCLUDING STYLE ELEMENTS, SKILL METHODZ, MASSIVE MONKEES, ROCK FORCE, GROUND ZERO AND DYNAMIC ROCKERS AND OUR CHAMPS' HOST, CRAZY LEGS, THE BIRTHPLACE OF B-BOY IS ALWAYS GOING TO BRING SOMETHING SPECIAL TO THE EVENT.

REST OF THE WORLD

WHILE THE USA AND THE UK WERE ORIGINAL DRIVING FORCES IN B-BOYING, COUNTRIES LIKE FRANCE, KOREA, JAPAN AND RUSSIA HAVE ALL BEEN PUTTING NEW FIRE INTO THE DISCIPLINE; AND YEAR ON YEAR MORE NATIONS ARE PUTTING THE TOP B-BOY NATIONS TO THE TEST. BELOW IS JUST A TASTE OF THE AMAZING INTERNATIONAL TALENT KEEPING THE B-BOY FLAME WELL AND TRULY BURNING...

GERMANY

In the early nineties, Germany was responsible for keeping b-boying firmly alive and kicking in Europe with the legendary event Battle of the Year which has been going for over 20 years. At the B-Boy Championships, German crews have repped since '97. South Side Rockers, Five Amox and most recently Style Crax have all battled at the Champs.

CANADA

Canadian crews have a long and illustrious history in breaking, and in 1999 Bag Of Trix Crew came and took the World Crew title, cementing their place in the Champs' history. In 2004 the Supernaturalz competed, losing out in an epic battle against Team Korea. Supernats member Dyzee is now pioneering a new judging system, which promises more clarity and consistency in judging b-boy battles.

SCANDINAVIA

Lots of great crews from Scandinavia have battled at the B-Boy Champs. Ghost Crew from Sweden/Finland, Natural Effects from Denmark and Flow Mo Crew have all made their mark. Flow Mo are Finland's most successful and long-standing crew. They are the most visible ambassadors of b-boying in their home city of Helsinki, establishing a world renowned dance studio called Saiffa. Their star dancer, b-boy Focus, is known for his incredible footwork and musicality winning the footwork battle two years running in 2007 and 2008.

HOLLAND

Holland is a hotbed of talent right now, a fact illustrated by their countries participation in the last three B-Boy Championships. Hustle Kidz, ADHD, Rugged Solutions and The Extraordinary Gentlemen (EXG) have blazed a trail, taking major honours across the world in both crews and solos. Hustle Kidz are Holland's reigning Champions and boast solo star b-boy Menno who won the World Solo Title at the Champs in 2008. Rugged Solutions have Niek Trann, aka JustDoIt, who was runner up at the Red Bull BC One event, and SkyChief, the reigning Benelux solo Champ. Most recently EXG have stood out for their energy, generated by their passion for the music.

BELGIUM

Super G took the solo title in 2002 and Belgium breakers have repped at the Champs regularly over the years, including Dynamics crew, and most recently Team Schmetta, who are one of the most consistent crews in Europe. The qualifiers held Bruxelles is always a hard-fought battle and is supported by Phil One and the Zulu Nation.

SPAIN/PORTUGAL

Barcelona Addictos put Spanish breaking firmly on the b-boy map, but Spain also has Fusion Rockers, Fresh Shit and Lunaticks who most recently won the Spain/Portugal qualifiers. The crew boasts one of the world's top b-girls, Movie One, who has redefined the perception of female breaking with her hard battling and dope style. Portugal's b-boy scene is up and coming with Momentum crew leading the way. Max, the leader of the crew organises the Eurobattle, an annual festival of dance held in Porto, which also plays host to the Spain/Portugal qualifiers for the B-Boy Champs.

EASTERN EUROPE

This vast region is producing some of the most exciting breaking at present. The crews are many and varied. Apart from Top 9, Russia also has All The Most, Back To Skool, and Funk Fanatix. Ukrainian crews Ruffneck Attack and Eastside

b-boys have battled at the B-Boy Championships, as have members from South Front b-boys.

SOUTH AMERICA

As you'd expect, Brazilian breaking mixes capoeira flips with breaking moves to create an original Brazilian flavour. In 2010, Amazon Crew from Brazil was the first South American crew to battle at the Championships.

CHINA

As well as long-standing crews like Forbidden City Break Rock, China has some exciting talent like 36 Chambers Crew emerging. They were the first Chinese crew to have participated in the UK Championships World Finals.

PROMOTERS' STORY

Tyrone & Mario Bee (Holland): 45 Live Company/promoters of The Notorious IBE

It was the mid eighties when we first saw breakdancing. Both us were 10-11 years old and learning the dance moves from our neighbourhood friends and off television. However, with only two Dutch TV channels at that time, chances of seeing breakdance on TV were fairly small, so instead we tuned in on German and British television. In those days both German and British TV occasionally showed movies like Beat Street, Wild Style, Style Wars or clips of local dance scenes.

In the late eighties, the hip-hop craze faded quickly in the Netherlands. It took about ten years for breakdance to grow again. Around 1997 we got active by organising small events and performing shows and workshops. At the time, breakdancing in Europe was really happening in Germany and France, but to us the UK was still an original hip-hop nation. It was the first European country for hip-hop to land in, and ever since the only country that could match the quality of US hip-hop. In the Netherlands there was a very large group of hip-hop lovers that had a greater love for British rappers, producers, DJs and graffiti writers than for the popular artists coming out of the US. Our love for UK breakdancing lay with crews like Broken Glass, UK Rock Steady, Second to None and the images of massive hip-hop events like UK Fresh and the UK B-Boy Championships.

Mario Bee and a little group of Dutch dancers visited the UK B-Boy Championships for the first time in 1999. It was a real experience. All of us back home were so happy that they made it into the intro of the official UK Champs 1999 video. It showed them in the middle of the legendary UK Champs queue at the Brixton Academy, having Mario Bee joking that they were the 'weed smokers from Holland' visiting the Champs. It all made such a big impression on us.

In 2000 Tyrone had his first encounter with the UK B-Boy Championships. At that time we were organising growing events like The Notorious IBE, Dutch B-Boy Championships and a hip-hop festival called Planet Rock in the city of Eindhoven. The Planet Rock festival took place in the same weekend as the UK B-Boy Champs and both of us wanted the German crew 5 Amox to be part of our events. I contacted Hooch and we agreed on having 5 Amox battle in Eindhoven on Saturday and travel to London to battle at the Champs on Sunday. It was a crazy operation but it worked. From that moment we started to work together to share artists or to have, say, upcoming b-boy Mouse or a UK crew to be part of our events in the Netherlands.

The cooperation between us and Hooch intensified in 2007. Our biggest international event The Notorious IBE had lost its venue and wasn't going to take place that year. It was Hooch that suggested we host a room at the first day of the Champs and name it the IBE room where we could host our own seven2smoke and footwork

battles. One year later when The Notorious IBE returned, Hooch hosted his room at The Notorious IBE presenting the first edition of the UK Champs European Finals.

Over the past few years we've not only come to work together for our events (IBE and UK Champs) but also started to cooperate more with our companies. Now almost weekly we share our ideas and views on the b-boy scene and try to come up with new concepts, events and methods of organisation that will give b-boying a bright future.

We could never have imagined that from visiting the UK Champs back in 1999 we would come to this point where we are now actually helping to shape the UK B-Boy Championships for the coming years. People always say nice words to each other about working together when all they really seek is personal profit; I think we have shown that you can both work together as a team and be successful. Our city, Rotterdam, is called 'the worker city'. Its slogan is 'action speaks louder than words', I think the same can be said about Hooch and the Champs.

DOS & DON'TS

DEYDEY

DO:

... be yourself; don't compete. And learn the basics.

DON'T:

... copy moves; it's not enough.

HONG 10

DO:

... practise.

DON'T:

... copy others.

MENNO

DO:

... stay yourself.

DON'T:

... bite! Don't be a groupie; be that hungry guy who's thinking, 'Give me some years and I will smoke you!!'

MOUSE

DO:

... stay focused and keep re-inventing yourself.

DON'T:

... do politics.

MORRIS

DO:

... find your own way of moving. Character is big in this game.

DON'T:

... think you invented anything without doing your homework or learning your history. Cats these days think they made everything!

PHYSICX (HYO GEUN KIM)

DO:

... what you want to do - either that will be a good thing or a bad thing. You should try everything out and learn from the experience. It's good to be adventurous and try new things.

DJ RENEGADE

DO:

... your research: find out what you're getting into. Some people think b-boying is about whatever they want it to be, and don't understand it has a history and a culture. You don't have to buy into it, but you do have to understand it.

DON'T:

... think you know more than you do! Keep your opinions to yourself until you know what you're talking about.

DJ SKEME RICHARDS

DO:

... your homework on being original.

DON'T:

... bite my style or I will have to call you out and make an example of you!

ROXY

DO:

... be yourself, ie learn foundation and evolve it the way you want.

DON'T:

... get caught up in the politics!

SALAH

DO:

... show who you are through your dancing.

DON'T:

... feel the beat: BE the beat .

J SMOOTH

DO:

... have clean technique. Clean means it has more visual impact for people watching you.

DON'T:

... try too hard; the musicality should just be inside you.

TEKNYC

DO:

... know your history.

DON'T:

... disrespect your elders.

TUF TIM TWIST

DO:

... go to New York City at least once.

DON'T:

... talk s*** on the internet.

VENUM

DO:

... your homework! Study the who's who of breakin' and know the foundation; it is the key for creativity and growth. In order to know where you can take the dance, you must know where it has been.

DON'T:

... dance for recognition or validity; do it because you love it and want to cultivate your skills for your own personal gratification, not to impress an audience.

WORLD B-BOY CREW CHAMPIONS

2010. Vagabonds (France)

2009. Endangered Species (USA)

2008. Top 9 (Russia)

2007. T.I.P. (Korea)

2006. Pokemon (France)

2005. Drifterz (Korea)

2004. Project Soul (Korea)

2003. Methods Of Havik (USA)

2002. Project Corea (Korea)

2001. USA All-Stars (USA)

2000. Suicidal Lifestyle (Hungary)

1999. Bag Of Trix (Canada)

1998. Spartanic Rockers (Japan)

1997. Second To None (UK)

1996. Second To None (UK)

WORLD SOLO B-BOY CHAMPIONS

2010. Flying Buddah (Russia)

2009. Morris (USA)

2008. Kosto (Russia)

2007. Menno (Holland)

2006. Mouse (UK)

2005. Roxrite (USA)

2004. Physicx (Korea)

2003. Ronnie Ruen (USA)

2002. Super G (Belgium)

2001. Sonic (Denmark)

2000. NOT HELD

1999. Tim Twist (UK)

1998. Evo (UK)

1997. Evo (UK)

1996. Evo (UK)

WORLD POPPING CHAMPIONS

2010. Nelson (France)

2009. DeyDey (France)

2008. Gucchon (Japan)

2007. Salah (France)

2006. J Smooth (USA)

2005. Iron Mike (France)

2004. Saly Sly (France)

WORLD LOCKING CHAMPIONS

2010. Flockey & Rae (Germany)

2009. A Train & Razzle Dazzle (Sweden)

2008. Lock & Lol (Korea)

2007. Miho & Yumi (Japan)

2006. The GoGo Brothers (Japan)

2005. Hilty & Bosch (Japan)

DJ LEACY CHIEF ROCKA AWARD WINNERS

2010. Mounir (France)

2009. Lil Jon (USA)

2008. Morris (USA)

2007. Differ (Korea)

2006. Hong 10 (Korea)

2005. Lilou (France)

FOOTWORK BATTLE WINNERS

2010. Kid Glyde (USA)

2009. Robin (Russia)

2008. Focus (Finland)

2007. Focus (Finland)

SEVEN 2 SMOKE BATTLE WINNERS

2010. Gravity (USA)

2009. Sunni (UK)

2008. Thumba (Finland)

B-GIRL BATTLE WINNERS

2010. Roxy, Eros, J - Kay (UK)

2009. Taija, AT, Candy (Finland & USA)

2008. Aruna, Kimi, Bo (Holland)

PHOTOGRAPHY

Raelene Begley: p 83
Steve Bonhage: pp 41, 183, 184
Cleve: pp 113-114, 118-119
Danny Fitzpatrick: p 20
(second from left)
Paul Hampartsoumian: p 20, 49, 50-51, 80, 82, 86, 164, 171
Jay McLaughlin: pp 13, 29, 32-33, 60, 74-75, 77, 90, 91-92, 99-100, 107-8, 140, 141, 159, 161, 170, 175, 178, 179
Maurice Meijs: 35, 84, 102, 121, 124-5, 130
Naki (www.naki.co.uk): 4, 9, 15, 20, 28, 29, 31, 34, 39, 40, 41 (bottom), 54-55, 56, 57, 58, 65, 66, 67, 68-9, 70-71, 78, 79, 81, 85, 87, 93-4, 97-8, 101, 109, 110, 111, 127, 130, 133, 136-7, 138, 143, 145, 146, 147, 151, 153, 157, 158, 172, 181
Stuart Nicolls: pp 52-53
Gary Salter: pp 10-11, 18-19, 24-25, 36-37, 44-45, 154-155, p 166-167

Every effort has been made to trace and acknowledge all photographers, but we apologise for any errors or omissions.